DARKNESS

Liam O'Flaherty

Liam O'Flaherty

DARKNESS

Brian Ó Conchubhair
EDITOR

ARLEN
HOUSE

Darkness

is published in 2014 by
ARLEN HOUSE
42 Grange Abbey Road
Baldoyle
Dublin 13
Ireland
Phone/Fax: 353 86 8207617
Email: arlenhouse@gmail.com

Distributed internationally by
SYRACUSE UNIVERSITY PRESS
621 Skytop Road, Suite 110
Syracuse, NY 13244–5290
Phone: 315–443–5534/Fax: 315–443–5545
Email: supress@syr.edu

978–1–85132–050–9, paperback
978–1–85132–074–5, hardback

Typesetting: Arlen House
Cover Images: Harry Kernoff
reproduced by kind courtesy of the artist's estate

CONTENTS

ACKNOWLEDGEMENTS

Pegeen O'Flaherty; Sheila Lahr-Leslie; Marion Hutton, Michael Mitzman, Arnold Paucker, Bob Davenport (William Roberts Society); Louise Morgan (National Gallery of Ireland); Honoria Faul (National Library of Ireland); Professor Nollaig Mac Congáil (NUI Galway); Professor Pádraig Ó Siadhail (St. Mary's University, Halifax); Mary O'Donoghue (Babson College); Professor Philip O'Leary (Boston College); Lochlann Ó Tuairisc, Micheál Ó Conghaile (CIC); Professor Robert Savage (Boston College); Chantelle Snyder (University of Notre Dame); Marie Darmody; Dr Ríona Nic Congáil (St. Patrick's College, DCU); Sara B. Weber, Kenneth Kinslow, Denise J. Massa (Hesburgh Library, University of Notre Dame); Kieran Hoare, Geraldine Curtin (James Hardiman Library, NUI Galway); Gordon E. Hogg, James Birchfield, Matthew Harris (Margaret I. King, Kentucky University); Kathleen Williams (John J. Burns Library, Boston College); Steven Johns (libcom); Ted Fox (Notre Dame), Dr Liam Ó Páircín (University of Limerick); Dr Caitríona Ó Torna (Rannóg an Aistriúcháin); Mary Jo Young (Notre Dame); Shane Mac Thomáis (Glasnevin Trust); Theodora Hannan, Dr Deirdre Ní Chonghaile, Seán Seosamh Ó Conchubhair and Tara MacLeod.

This project was completed with the assistance of a Naughton Fellowship from the Keough-Naughton Institute for Irish Studies, University of Notre Dame. My thanks to Professor Máire Ní Annracháin and Professor Liam Mac Mathúna, Scoil na Gaeilge, an Léinn Cheiltigh, Bhéaloideas Éireann agus na Teangeolaíochta, an Coláiste Ollscoile, Baile Átha Cliath.

IMAGE ACKNOWLEDGEMENTS

Liam O'Flaherty, courtesy of Pegeen O'Flaherty
Charles Lahr (libcom.org)
Liam O'Flaherty by William Roberts (William Roberts Society)
Sarah Roberts by William Roberts (William Roberts Society)
Esther Archer by William Roberts (William Roberts Society)
Rhys John Davies at Penn Hotel, 1939. World Telegram staff photographer Al Aumuller, Library of Congress Prints and Photographs Division, Washington DC.
Shelia Leslie: Photographs of Charles Lahr and Esther Archer
The anonymous owner of the Harry Kernoff images for permission to reproduce them here.

The editor and publisher gratefully acknowledge permission granted to reproduce copyright material in this book. Every effort has been made to trace copyright holders and obtain permission for the use of copyrighted material. The publisher regrets any errors or omissions and would be grateful if notified of any corrections that should be incorporated in future editions of this book.

Private Cornelius Guinness
3492, 2nd Bn. Royal Munster Fusiliers, British Army
Born: 55 Fair Lane, Cork – 14 September 1871
Died: Etreux, Picardie, France – 27 August 1914

Commandant Pat O'Connor
O/C 2nd Bn. Kerry No. 1 Brigade, IRA
Born: Rathmorrell, Causeway – 5 March 1896
Died: Adelaide, Australia – 5 February 1934

DARKNESS

Liam O'Flaherty

INTRODUCTION:
SHEDDING LIGHT ON LIAM O'FLAHERTY'S *DARKNESS*

So much of what is important in writing and publishing happens offstage. Writers struggle with their work, literary patrons boost aspiring authors, manuscripts are passed from one editor to another, submissions are rejected, negotiations come to nothing, all without leaving traces in print.

– Christopher Hilliard 2006, 39.

An bundráma ba chonspóidí dár léirigh an Comhar sna blianta luatha seo *Dorchadas* (1926), tráigéide chumasach dhuairc suite ar Oileán Árann le Liam Ó Flaithearta. An fhionaíl, agus na mothúcháin taobh thiar di, ábhar an dráma a raibh atmaisféar gruama aige tríd síos. Sa léiriú, bhí roinnt macallaí ciana le cluinstin ó laethanta achrannacha Synge.

– Pádraig Ó Siadhail 1993, 65.

Yeats, in all reaction, set himself, as did Joyce and O'Flaherty from a differing perspective, to critique the idea that time moves ever and progressively on. To these writers, diversion was the way. Their improvisations formed an alternative public sphere whose instruments were not the court and parliaments, but the theatre, protests, open letters, visions, broadsides and little magazines that gave the avant-garde spectral life in the controversy that was Ireland after empire.

– Nicholas Allen 2009, 88.

Portrait of Liam O'Flaherty (1954)
Harry Kernoff, RHA (1900–1974)
Pastel on Paper, 18" x 15"/45.5 x 38cm

Liam O'Flaherty, Author (1933)
Harry Kernoff, RHA (1900–1974)
Oil on Panel, 20" x 15"/51 x 38cm

Dorchadas was, and remains, an aberration – an original Irish-language play rather than a translation from English or French, a tragedy rather than a comedy or farce. Its author, a native Irish-speaker rather than a cultural nationalist learner of the language, was a successful and popular English-language author, an Irish Volunteer and World War I veteran, a committed republican and anti-Treatyite, a Civil War combatant, and a socialist who reputedly espoused Nietzschean notions and harboured anti-Catholic credentials. Published in English in England and the United States in non-orthodox publications, the text was rejected in Ireland for publication in Irish.

The story of *Dorchadas* and its English-language translation *Darkness* is the story of Irish cultural and literary affairs in the early years of the Free State. It presents an anti-iconic image of the *Gaeltacht*, the Irish-speaking heartland and presumed reservoir of 'Irishness', and concerns two of the most important and impressive state-sponsored initiatives and nation-building projects undertaken during the Free State era to popularize the Irish language and its culture: An Gúm and An Comhar Drámaíochta. The drama's production, its popular and critical reception, and its clandestine and aborted publication in Irish reveal the visceral stresses and emotional strains of constitutional, cultural and linguistic politics in the Irish Free State. The series of events surrounding *Dorchadas* lays bare the animosities and simmering tensions bequeathed by the Civil War and reveals escalating Catholic middle-class expectations of propriety and decorum in language, literature and behaviour in the newly-established Irish Free State. Furthermore, it is the story of two of the most significant Irish-language authors of the period: Liam O'Flaherty and Pádraic Ó Conaire.

The play's subsequent translation and publication in English challenges notions of intellectual isolation within the Irish language, pointing to an often-ignored and submerged strand within Irish-language literature and elucidating the rapid exchange of information and ideas in early twentieth-century Europe. It was in this environment that an Irish-speaker from the Aran Islands could collaborate with avowed English, Indian, Welsh, and German socialists and anarchists, as well as prestigious artists, writers and intellectuals, and American publishers and pornographers.

Darkness, the English-language translation of *Dorchadas*, engineered a convergence and intersection of World War I veterans, anarchists, socialists and avant-garde artists. With increasing levels of separation, it also links An Comhar Drámaíochta and the Gaelic League/Conradh na Gaeilge to *Blast*, William Roberts, Wyndham Lewis and the British Vorticists, and, to a lesser extent, Samuel Roth, aka 'the Pirate Roth'.

Simultaneously, *Darkness* illustrates that modernism, socialism and communism were global concerns in the interwar period, transcending linguistic zones, regional divides and national boundaries. Such concerns gave rise to discourses in which O'Flaherty and Ó Conaire were both au fait and fluent. Indeed, O'Flaherty's project – in tandem with Pádraic Ó Conaire, a committed socialist – to use theatre as a means of educating and sensitizing rural Irish-speakers in the *Gaeltachtaí* speaks to Wyndham Lewis' modernist understanding of art as a seductive, potentially political and moral force (Tuma, 1987, 406).

Pádraic Ó Conaire (1882–1928)

O'Flaherty and Ó Conaire, in their rejection of the status quo and their proposed joint endeavour to produce a series of Irish-language plays for a touring theatre, mirror British modernists' rejection of Victorian society and the publishing industry's narrow morality in favour of groups, 'gangs', coteries and clubs (Thacker 2010, 689–90). Both O'Flaherty and Ó Conaire, at different times in their lives, attempted to establish, in Raymond Williams' terms, a 'cultural formation' – a loose affiliation of like-minded friends – to promote artistic and intellectual development and to ignore, overthrow or reform the institutions they considered inimical to that purpose. The proposed theatrical touring group represents

> part of the more multifaceted scenario governing how cultural formations emerge and organize themselves in order to get their voices heard, perhaps dethatching (sic) themselves from certain mainstream aspects of culture, only to re-emerge with other aspects of commercial culture and thus compromise some of their own artistic rhetoric (Thacker 2010, 690–1).

Dorchadas and *Darkness* therefore provide a prism that allows a reading of O'Flaherty and Ó Conaire not only as participants in Irish-language modernism and revivalism but also as participants in the wider global literary, political, and cultural concerns of socialist, communist, feminist, women's rights and left-wing political movements.

In this light, O'Flaherty and Ó Conaire escape from the rigid interpretations demanded by narrow forms of nationalism and shine in a newer, bolder, fuller spectrum illustrating Lloyd's argument that the various major movements involved in the 1913–1922 Irish political and cultural ferment moved at 'different paces'. Such movements, he writes, are often occluded by subsequent history's focus on political institutions and state apparatuses. Yet very often these movements were neither:

> (E)ntirely absorbed or otherwise dissolved in the hegemony of state-orientated nationalisms but sustained by dedicated individuals and minority groups. As a result they persist as distinct elements of the struggle or as recalcitrant tendencies for the state. But they do so, not as particles of the prehistory of nationalism awaiting absorption, but as active constituents of the modern, inflected just as is nationalism by recent history, though with different ends and correspondingly different narratives (Lloyd 1999, 28–33).

O'Flaherty and Ó Conaire represent such distinct elements within cultural nationalism and within Irish-language literature. The story of *Dorchadas* and *Darkness* is the story of an alternative vision, a challenge to conservatism and propriety. Tracing its history offers a unique insight into the intersecting worlds of international socialism, modernism, anarchism and political radicalism and reveals obscured facets of the diverse and multifaceted nature of Irish-language discourse, as well as the highly nuanced political and cultural psychologies of Free State Ireland. These realities, it appears, remain largely understudied and undervalued.

Dorchadas, ultimately, is a story of failure. It is the story of the eclipse of a socialist and modernist theatre project in the early years of the Free State. Yet in a counterfactual narrative, one can speculate on the impact of a touring theatre troupe in *Gaeltacht* regions performing O'Flaherty/Ó Conaire plays directed by Gearóid Ó Lochlainn, Micheál Mac Liammóir and Hilton Edwards, including the consternation it may – and most likely would – have raised. *Dorchadas* conveyed confidence, boldness, innovation and ambition. It represented critical, cutting-edge Irish-language drama: a challenging, self-examining, self-reflective mode, not subservient to cultural nationalism or Catholic dogma, not adhering blindly to stereotypes, platitudes or nation-building aspirations. It offered a jolt to those comfortable with the image they typically saw of themselves and their culture in Irish-language productions, both theatrical and textual, in the same way O'Casey challenged Irish nationalist history in *The Plough and the Stars*, which was produced on the Abbey stage on 8 February 1926, less than a month before *Dorchadas* appeared in the same venue. It demolished the iconoclastic stereotypes of female agency and the prescribed role of women in post-revival Free State Ireland that dominated contemporary Irish-language drama, answering the call for modern Irish-language drama issued by Patrick Pearse some twenty years earlier:

> This is the 20th century; and no literature can take root in the 20th century which is not of the 20th century. We want no Gothic revival. We would have the problems of today fearlessly dealt with in Irish; the loves and hates

and desires and doubts of modern men and women. The drama of the land war; the tragedy of the emigration mania; the stress and poetry and comedy of the language movement; the pathos and vulgarity of Anglo-Ireland; the abounding interest of Irish politics; the relations of priests to people; the perplexing education riddle; the drink evil; the increase in lunacy; such social problems as (say) the loveless marriage; these are matters which loom large in our daily lives, which build considerably in our daily conversations; but we find not the faintest echoes of them in the Irish books that are being written. There would seem to be an amazing conspiracy among our writers to refrain absolutely from dealing with life, the one thing which, properly considered, literature has any concern! (Pearse, 1906).

The revival narrative's prescribed roles, for women and men, were essential to allow the nationalist credo to successfully challenge the colonial narrative that had denationalized and demeaned the native culture over several centuries. In both *Dorchadas* and *Darkness*, O'Flaherty contradicted the coherent narrative that prescribed Free State women to the home and hearth as passive, disengaged reproducers of national identity, devoid of sexual freedom, sexual choice, authority and public voice. Critics were not slow to recognize its newness, even if labelling it proved difficult. As a *Fáinne an Lae* critic declared, *Dorchadas* was new and challenging, something Irish audiences would have to become accustomed to as Irish-language drama developed and matured. As with much, if not most, of O'Flaherty's fiction it explores the cost and loss involved in pursuing an attempt to attain freedom and personal fulfilment, even if that entails violating social expectation and communal laws.

LIAM O'FLAHERTY

William Flaherty was born on 28 August 1896, the second male child to Michael (Maidhc) Ó Flaithearta and Margaret (Maggie) Ganly, in Gort na gCapall, Inis Mór, the largest of the three Aran Islands in Galway Bay. Ruth Dudley Edwards advances the notion that O'Flaherty was brought up in great poverty and insecurity in Gort na gCapall, where inhabitants lived in terror of famine, disease and eviction (Dudley Edwards 2011, 59).

Liam O'Flaherty

The 1901 census records his father as a 56-year-old labourer and farmer who shared his home with his wife, Margaret (44 years), and six children at the onset of the new century: Julia (16), Annie (12), Thomas (10), Bridget (7), Willie (4), and Agnes (1). The family, Catholic and bilingual, resided in a three-room settlement of the 'second grade'.[1] The youngest boy, Willie attended the local National School at Oatquarter beginning in 1902, coming under the influence of the Limerick-man David O'Callaghan, who taught on the island from 1885–1911 (Costello 1996, 15) until his dispute with, and ultimate dismissal by, the notorious Fr Farragher (McMahon 2008, 54–61).

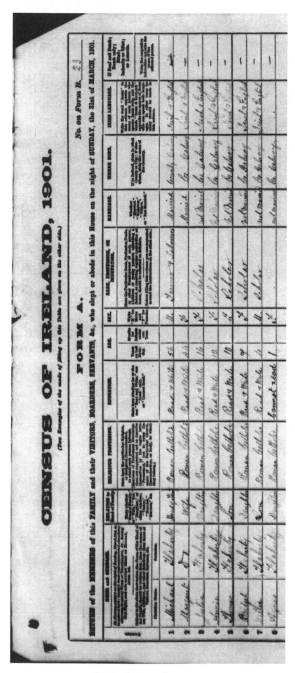

1901 Census Return

CENSUS OF IRELAND, 1911.

Two Examples of the mode of filling up this Table are given on the other side.

FORM A.

No. on Form B. ___

RETURN of the MEMBERS of this FAMILY and their VISITORS, BOARDERS, SERVANTS, &c., who slept or abode in this House on the night of SUNDAY, the 2nd of APRIL, 1911.

Number	NAME AND SURNAME		RELATION to Head of Family.	RELIGIOUS PROFESSION.	EDUCATION.	AGE (last Birthday) and SEX.		RANK, PROFESSION, OR OCCUPATION.	PARTICULARS AS TO MARRIAGE.					WHERE BORN.	IRISH LANGUAGE.	If Deaf and Dumb; Dumb only; Blind; Imbecile or Idiot; or Lunatic.
	Christian Name.	Surname.	State whether "Head of Family," or "Wife," "Son," "Daughter," or other Relative; "Visitor," "Boarder," "Servant," &c.	State here the particular Religion, or Religious Denomination, to which each person belongs. [Members of Protestant Denominations are requested not to describe themselves by the vague term "Protestant," but to enter the name of the Particular Church, Denomination, or Body to which they belong.]	State here whether he or she can "Read and Write," can "Read" only, or "Cannot Read."	Ages of Males.	Ages of Females.	State the particular Rank, Profession, Trade, or other Employment of each person. Children or young persons attending a School, or receiving regular instruction at home, should be returned as Scholars. [No entry should be made in the case of wives, daughters, or other female relatives solely engaged in domestic duties at home.] Before filling this column you are requested to read the instructions on the other side.	Whether "Married," "Widower," "Widow," or "Single."	State for each Married Woman entered on this Schedule the number of— Completed years the present Marriage has lasted. If less than one year, write "under one."	Total Children born alive.	Children still living.		If in Ireland, state in what County or City. If elsewhere, state the name of the Country.	Write the word "Irish" in this column opposite the name of each person who speaks Irish only, and the words "Irish & English" opposite the names of those who can speak both languages. In other cases no entry should be made in this column.	Write the respective infirmities opposite the name of the afflicted person.
	1.		3.	4.	5.	6.	7.	8.	9.	10.	11.	12.		13.	14.	15.
1	John	Slattery	Head of Family	Roman Catholic	Read + write	66		Farmer	Married					Co. Kildare	Irish + English	
2	Margaret	Slattery	wife	Roman Catholic	Read + write		56		Married	59	14	11		Co. Galway	Irish & English	
3	James	Slattery	son	Roman Catholic	Read + write	20		Farmers son	Single					Co. Kildare	Irish & English	
4	Agnes	Slattery	daughter	Roman Catholic	Read + write		12	Scholar	Single					Co. Galway	Irish & English	
5																

1911 Census Return

24

It was O'Callaghan, O'Flaherty later claimed, who inspired his interest in the island's vernacular language despite his father's disdain (O'Flaherty 1927, 348). Intended as a postulant to 'be trained as a priest for the conversion of African negroes to the Roman Catholic religion' (Mac an Iomaire 2001, 27) and guided by Fr Thomas Naughton, a Holy Ghost priest who frequented Aran, O'Flaherty enrolled at Rockwell College in County Tipperary in 1908. A dispute with the college's authorities prompted his transfer, as a lay student, in 1913 to Blackrock College in the Dublin coastal suburbs (Sheeran 1976, 56–64; Costello 1996, 21–23). The political ferment of the times led him to correspond with Eoin Mac Neill who sanctioned him to form a troop of the Irish Volunteers among the senior boys, a move that endeared O'Flaherty neither to college authorities nor to the Redmondite parents (Costello 1996, 23). He studied for a term in Holy Cross College, Clonliffe, and spent an additional period pursuing the classics at University College Dublin, where once again he attempted to form a Volunteer unit (Costello 1996, 25–26). While at Clonliffe, he would have participated in college rituals:

> (w)hose denizens were marked out in UCD by their black suits, furled umbrellas and the bowler hats that were the butt of ridicule and practical jokes. Not only did the students have to walk in pairs for forty minutes through the Dublin streets every day, but on alternate Sundays, to the merriment of local urchins, they walked to the Pro-Cathedral in Marlborough Street to assist at High Mass, dressed in soutane and soprana (a black wool cloak lined with red silk) and with Roman hats with wide, circular brims lined with white silk ... For leisure, he and other students often visited the enormous brothel quarter that had made Dublin the red-light capital of Europe (Dudley Edwards 2011, 60).

Discarding any lingering hopes of an ordination, he enlisted as a private soldier, registration number 10929, in the Second Battalion, Irish Guard, on St Brigit's Day, 1916 under his mother's maiden name – William Ganly – as World War I entered its second year (BNA, File WO/372/7).

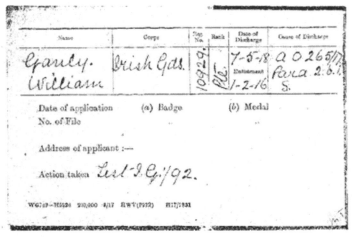

William Ganly's Military Record

Billeted at Caterham, Surrey, for initial training, William Ganly was subsequently deployed to the front in January 1917. He incurred injury during a bombardment at Langemarch as part of the third Battle of Ypres in September 1917. His convalescence at various military hospitals included a year in King George V's Hospital – now St Bricin's Military Hospital, Infirmary Road, Arbour Hill, Dublin – which housed a special neurological unit for troops identified in other Irish hospitals. He was discharged from the army on 7 May 1918, but would suffer bouts of depression throughout his life and remained susceptible to loud noise.

Following the Great War, he travelled the world and, if his own accounts are to be believed, frequented various locations in North and South America, especially Cuba, as well as Europe. He developed an interest in socialism, communism and the Industrial Workers of the World, before returning to Ireland in 1921:

> After a period in Aran musing 'on the indefinability of the paregoric, the uncertainty of life, and the constant tribulation to be met in the world', in late 1921 he joined the febrile left in Dublin, editing and selling the *Workers' Republic* on the streets, trying vainly to persuade the party to back workers who were seizing workplaces and setting up soviets, and organising the Dublin unemployed – many of whom were ex-servicemen (Dudley Edwards 2011, 67).

In the wake of the Irish Free State's declaration on 7 December 1921, O'Flaherty, acting as 'chairman' of the Unemployed Committee, seized[2] the Rotunda's Concert Hall and Pillar Room (now the Gate Theatre) on 18 January 1922.[3] The committee unfurled a red flag and issued a proclamation calling for a Workers' Republic, but their initiative failed to generate public support or sympathy; they abandoned the building after two days.

The Rotunda

O'Flaherty fled to Cork where the electorate had empowered a Sinn Féin-Transport Workers' coalition (Allen 2009, 16) but returned in June to participate, on the Anti-Treaty Republican side, in the Battle of Dublin.[4] It is believed he was present in Vaughan's Hotel (Fox 1943, 236) when Republicans seized and held the Four Courts and several city centre hotels, including Vaughan's (Parnell Square), Moran's Hotel and Hammam's Turkish Baths (O'Connell Street), between 28 June and 5 July 1922. A rumour circulated that he had been shot and killed on Capel Street but proved unfounded. Still alive, he saw the Free State forces attack, and recapture, O'Connell Street before fleeing the city on 9 July for England, where he focused on fiction rather than fighting.

The New Leader published his first short story, 'The Sniper' – authored by William O'Flaherty – on 12 January 1923, and Cape published his first novel, *Thy Neighbour's Wife*, later that same year. He returned to Dublin at the onset of March 1924 and soon settled in Wicklow. *Spring Sowing* (Cape) and *The Black Soul* (Cape) appeared later that year when he cofounded The Radical Club with Francis Stuart; the club's initial membership included Cecil Salkeld, Austin Clarke, F.R. Higgins, Brinsley MacNamara, Pádraig Ó Conaire, Harry Kernoff and other distinguished writers and artists. It is thought that club member Cecil ffrench Salkeld arranged the subsidiary Radical Painters' Group where Harry Kernoff exhibited in 1926. Kernoff drew several portraits of O'Flaherty: 'Liam O'Flaherty, Author' (1933), 'A Portrait Study of Liam O'Flaherty on the Aran Islands' (1936), and 'Portrait of Liam O'Flaherty' (1954).

In November 1924 Eoin Ua Mathghamhna, writing in the Jesuit journal *The Irish Monthly*, identified

O'Flaherty as an obscene writer (Ua Mathghamhna 1924, 569–73). It was that year, at his height as an English-language writer that he had decided to begin writing professionally in Irish.[5] From May 1924 to September 1925, he published a poem and seven short stories in publications such as *Dublin Magazine* and the Irish-language weekly newspaper *Fáinne an Lae*. Cape published his Irish War of Independence-based thriller *The Informer* in 1925, a book for which he received the James Tait Black Memorial Prize.

1925 also saw the composition of his *Dorchadas* and marked his initial meeting and romantic involvement with Margaret Barrington, wife of Trinity College historian Edmund Curtis. His only known Irish-language play, *Dorchadas* was staged at the Abbey Theatre in 1926.

Mr. Gilhooley (Cape) appeared in 1926, as well, followed the next year by *The Life of Tim Healy* (Cape) and *The Fairy-Goose and Two Other Stories* (Faber & Gwyer). Nominated for the *Femina-Vie Heureuse* Prize for best fictional work of the year 1925–1926, *Mr. Gilhooley* caused a stir and, according to Costello, 'was as well-known, even as notorious, as Joyce's *Ulysses*. The text caused concern at his publishers, and later editions were expurgated' (Costello, 1996, 58). O'Flaherty published *The Assassin* (Cape) in 1928,[6] and in 1929 Arthur Robison directed *The Informer*, an 83-minute black-and-white film adaptation of O'Flaherty's novel.[7] *The Informer* was again turned into a movie in 1935 by his relative John Ford and was nominated for the Best Picture Oscar, only to lose out to *Mutiny on the Bounty*.[8] 1930 saw a foreword to *Six Cartoons* by Gal (Alfred Lowe), while 1932 brought an amicable divorce from Margaret Barrington and the publication of *Skerrett* (Victor Gollancz). O'Flaherty once again abandoned Ireland and took up residence in The Strand, London, and his autobiography *Shame the Devil* (Grayson & Grayson) appeared in 1934. Around that time he met Kitty Harding Tailer, who would become his life-long partner. Three years later he published *Famine* (Victor Gollancz) and *The Short Stories of Liam O'Flaherty* (Cape).

By 1940 he was living in the United States with Tailer, but he returned to Ireland in 1952 and took up residence at 9 Court Flats/Apartments, Wilton Place, close to the Grand Canal and Lower Baggot Street, which became his permanent home in Dublin.

View of Court Flats/Apartments, Wilton Place

Poster for *The Informer* (1935)

Movie poster: *The Informer*

Under the influence of Eoghan Ó hAnluain[9] and Breandán Ó hEithir, son of his sister Delia – 'the only other person on earth that understands me' (Kelly 1996, 33–34) – he returned to Irish; publishing, broadcasting and reviewing stories in that language. *Dúil*, a collection of old and new short stories, appeared in 1953, published by Sairséal & Dill in a print run of 2,500 copies, the first 500 of which the author signed. There were rumours of a work in progress titled *Corp agus Anam*, but such was not to be. O'Flaherty died on 7 September 1984, and, controversially,[10] a funeral service with Catholic rites was celebrated at University Church, Dublin, before his remains were cremated at Glasnevin Cemetery on Dublin's north side.

Breandán Ó hEithir (1930–1990)

THE COMPOSITION OF *DORCHADAS*

The circumstances surrounding the play's composition can be found in O'Flaherty's letters to Edward Garnett (1868–1937) – his friend, mentor, and patron[11] – and his 1927 letter to the *Irish Statesman*. O'Flaherty returned to Dublin in March 1924 and lodged at 12 South Circular Road, Portobello. It was around this time that he became a member of the United Arts Club, which had recently relocated to 3 Upper Fitzwilliam Street (Lynch 2011, 254), and frequented the Jammet family restaraunt in Dublin, which in 1926 relocated to 45–46 Nassau Street. As Dublin's only French restaurant, it hosted many of the city's leading writers and artists. On accepting an invitation to George Russell's home, he encountered Edmund Curtis (1881–1943), Professor of History at Trinity, and his wife, Margaret Barrington (1896–1982) – 'a very pretty young woman, fifteen years younger than the professor' (Kelly 1996, 73) whom he had married in 1922 in what was a *mariage blanc* (Costello 1996, 55). Later that month, O'Flaherty confided to Garnett that:

> The lady who is unfortunate enough to have conceived an affection for me here is also married and lives with her husband very dutifully. She belongs to an old Norman family, dark haired, shrewd, very cultivated and very passionate in a cold, feline kind of way. She is one of the most sought after beauties in Dublin, but she does not enthuse me, at least not very much. But she is good copy. At the moment her husband is away in England attending some affair or other, and tomorrow the two of us are going to tramp out into the country (Kelly 1996, 79).

In response to Garnett's unfavourable criticism of a story written by Barrington that O'Flaherty had sent him, O'Flaherty informed him: 'She herself is very interesting too, though a trifle conceited and parochial on account of her environment ...' (Kelly 1996, 83). By

3 April 1924, O'Flaherty crowed 'And I have secured the wife of Professor Curtis, which is, of course, the most important conquest!' (Kelly 1996, 81). Having visited his declining father in Aran during April, he provided Aldbury, Tring, Hertfordshire, north of London, as a postal address for himself and Margaret Barrington in June and July. At the end of July, he informed Garnett that Dublin is 'agog with story of our elopement' (Kelly 1996, 98). After spells in Dorset and London, they appeared in Sunny Bank Cottage, Great Milton, Oxfordshire, close to the university town, in October. During their stay in London, Edmund Curtis had met them and attempted to reunite with his wife. O'Flaherty recounted for Garnett how:

> He wanted her to go back to him and hummed and hawed about the impossibility of getting a divorce but I believe he will do so when he sees us back in Dublin next Spring. I told him we were going to come back there and he was astounded that I should have such a lack of feeling for him. Finally I got him to agree to a divorce should Margaret still wish to live with me after another six months. So there the matter stands. He's rather a decent man, though frightfully nervous and conscious of his own importance (Kelly 1996, 104–5).[12]

By early January 1925 O'Flaherty was residing at 16 Upper Mount Street, Dublin, but he relocated to Bray later that month and was excited at the prospect of moving into a rented cottage in Glencree.

Admidst such excitement and intrigue, O'Flaherty also came to befriend the leading Irish-language writer of the revival, a fellow Galway man and committed socialist, Pádraic Ó Conaire.[13] Despite O'Flaherty having his sister point the established author out to him at the 1913 Oireachtas cultural festival in Galway, the two Galway men had never met until Ó Conaire commended O'Flaherty's short story 'Bás na Bó', which appeared in *Fáinne an Lae*, to F.R. Higgins, who apparently facilitated an introduction.[14] In partnership with Pádraic Ó Conaire,[15] whom he described to Garnett as 'a good man and his countrymen are treating him very badly' (Kelly 1996, 123), O'Flaherty intended to produce an Irish-language travelling theatre troupe for which they would write a series of dramatic scripts. This approach, in their opinion, represented, according to O'Flaherty:

> (T)he best means of starting a new literature in Irish. I became fearfully enthusiastic. The two of us went to Dublin and entered a hall where some fellows were holding a Gaeltacht Commission. We put our scheme before them for a travelling theatre and so on. I guaranteed to write ten plays. They thought we were mad and, indeed, they took little interest in us. In fact, I could see by their looks and their conversation that they considered us immoral persons (*Irish Statesman* 1927, 348).[16]

The Gaeltacht Commission in question was founded in 1925 by the Cumann na nGaedheal government to inquire and report on the percentage of Irish speakers in any district, which would warrant such a district being regarded as a partly, or fully, Irish-speaking district. This commission was further charged with making recommendations as to the use of Irish in the administration of such districts and any possible steps to improve the inhabitants' economic condition (*Coimisiún na Gaeltachta* 1926, 1; see Walsh 2002; Ó Torna 2005). Undaunted, O'Flaherty composed *Dorchadas* in Irish and presented the script to Gearóid Ó Lochlainn[17] – doyen of the Irish-language theatre recently returned from Denmark – in the hope that he would direct it as a Comhar Drámaíochta production.

O'Flaherty, in a letter to Garnett dated July 1925, promised to translate and forward the text as soon as it was returned to him, even though he doubted its commercial appeal:

> I didn't hear about that play yet. As soon as I get hold of the manuscript again I'm going to rattle it off in English and send it to you. It's fine stuff I think, but as a play I am doubtful. Poetic plays hardly ever sell well. Even Synge's *Deirdre*, which is the most beautiful thing he wrote, acts badly (Kelly 1996, 124).

In July 1925, the courts in London granted a decree of *nisi* on the grounds of adultery in the Curtis' divorce proceedings; it became a decree of absolute in February 1926 (Costello 1996, 55 & 58). O'Flaherty duly informed Garnett that the newspapers had announced the divorce[18] and that An Comhar Drámaíochta was to produce *Dorchadas*:

> That piece I was telling you about was an Irish play. I finished it but I have no time to translate it into English, as I am throwing it to the wolves, i.e. the Irish Drama League. Let them produce it if they like. If not, I'll translate it. It's not a good play in the ordinary sense, but it's a good piece of writing and I fancy you would like it (Kelly 1996, 124).

At this juncture Esther Archer (aka Charles Lahr) wrote seeking a submission from O'Flaherty for the first edition of *The New Coterie*. Charles Lahr (1885–1971), born at Wendlesheim, Germany, had flirted as a teenager first with Buddhism and later anarchy. Deserting Germany for London in 1905 to avoid military conscription, he worked initially as a baker before being drawn more and more into socialist politics. As Charlie, rather than Karl or Charles, Lahr became a member and a frequent visitor of anarchist clubs and haunts in London and gradually came to the attention of the police, who focused not only on him but also on those to whom he rented rooms in his King's Cross house. As happened with many Germans and Austrians during World War I, he was interned at Alexandria Palace, London, from 1915 to 1919. On release, he continued to work for the International Workers of the World, where he first met Esther Argeband/Archer, his future wife.

Charles Lahr (1885–1971)

The Coterie, No 3, 1919

Esther Argeband/Archer (1898–1970)

Portrait of Esther Archer by William Roberts

At age 13, having left school, Esther Argeband worked at Rothman's cigarette factory in London's East End, where she became an organizer for the International Workers of the World. A member of Sylvia Pankhurst's Workers Socialist Federation, she developed a reputation as an open-air speaker but would later change her name to Archer to avoid anti-Semitic prejudice. She encountered Lahr at the Charlotte Street Socialist Club, and they married in 1922. Both joined the Communist Party in 1920 but left within a year.[19] It is suggested, however, that it was during this period that Lahr and O'Flaherty first met (Fox 1938; Goodway 1977). Esther bought a bookshop at 68 Red Lion Square, Holborn, that she subsequently ran as the Progressive Bookshop with Lahr. It soon became a focal point for authors and activists seeking radical publications.

K.S. Bhat,[20] author of several tracts on labour relations, proposed the newly married couple become managers of *The New Coterie – A Quarterly Magazine of Art and Literature*. Established in 1925 to replace the now defunct *The Coterie*, it maintained its predecessor's mission and ethos by serving readers seeking to be familiar with modern contemporary cultural and artistic trends. Esther was a close friend of Sarah Roberts, leading to several collaborations between their respective husbands, including Roberts providing artwork for *The New Coterie*.

Six editions appeared between November 1925 and Summer 1927, and the magazine would boast authors as distinguished as D.H. Lawrence, H.E. Bates, Rhys Davies, Aldous Huxley, T.F. Powys, Louis Golding, Geoffrey West and Faith Compton Mackenzie.

The post-war anti-German bias led Lahr to use his wife's name – Esther Archer or, more frequently, E. Archer – when the couple commenced publishing off-prints from the journal as independent booklets. O'Flaherty responded to Archer's initial request for submissions, and his 'Civil War' appeared in the first number of *The New Coterie* on November 25, 1925 (60–66).[21]

Shortly afterwards, Archer proposed publishing a limited signed edition of 100 copies of the story (Kelly 1996, 129 & 135). Anxious to generate any income, O'Flaherty agreed. He had experienced pecuniary peril and depression since early 1924, as he explained to Garnett in a letter from 16 Upper Mount Street:

> I am in a very low condition here and absolutely friendless – everybody has turned against me. I have no money. Would you ask Cape to purchase the copyrights of my four books for whatever he can give? (Kelly 1996, 111).

Charles Lahr outside the Progressive Bookshop,
68 Red Lion Square, Holborn

At the end of the same month, he again wrote to Garnett:

> I find myself snowed under with debt, with a shattered
> constitution and as many friends as a bailiff in the west of
> Ireland … I have appealed to my sister for funds. If she
> fails me I am damned (Kelly 1996, 111).[22]

Nor was this occasion the first in which he fretted over
finances. On receiving an invitation from Séamus
O'Sullivan[23] (1879–1958), editor of *The Dublin
Magazine*, on 14 March 1924, to publish in the journal,
he grumbled to Garnett:

> (t)he blighter has no money and he can only pay about a
> guinea a thousand. I could sell everything I will write for
> the next two years in Dublin within twenty four hours,
> but all I would get would be a guinea a thousand. They
> pay for politics in this country but they refuse to pay for
> literature, unless it is political literature (Kelly 1996, 76).

On 25 November 1925, O'Flaherty divulged to Garnett
that he was translating *Dorchadas* into English and
sending it to a literary agent in London. He bragged
about Ó Lochlainn's eagerness:

> I am now translating my play into English. They are very
> excited about it in Dublin, the Gaelic crowd. O'Loughlin,
> [Ó Lochlainn] who is going to produce it, is exceptionally
> enthusiastic. I am sending the English version to an agent
> in London. I wonder would you care to see it? (Kelly
> 1996, 136).

In early February 1926, O'Flaherty sent a letter to
Archer from 5 Upper Leeson Street, confirming his
impending trip to London and inquiring if his play
would be of interest to *The New Coterie* and as an
independent publication afterwards:

> Dear Comrade, … I am eagerly looking forward to my
> visit to London. I have a short play which I will bring to
> show you. You might like to use it for the next number of
> *New Coterie*, and then issue it as a booklet. It would go

very well. It's the best thing I have done. It's the only way to escape the public and make the bourgeoisie pay (Kelly 1996, 140–1).

On 20 March, after An Comhar Drámaíochta's production in the Abbey Theatre, he mailed the English-language text to Archer. O'Flaherty asked that the play, or even the first act, be read in order to establish his copyright and acquiesced to Archer's request for a sketching by the artist William Roberts:

> Dear Comrade ... I am sending the play *Darkness* under separate cover. Thanks for the copies of 'The Terrorist', you may use the play under those terms but if possible try and get it acted before printing it, so that I would not lose the dramatic rights. One act read in a drawing room would be sufficient I believe. Not that I expect it will ever be acted, but it's better to make sure, and it was a big stage success here in Irish. I am sure the drawing is all right, and it's very nice of Mr. Roberts to want to paint me (Kelly 1996, 144–45).

On 21 April 1926, O'Flaherty returned two dozen signed copies of Roberts' sketch to Archer and in addition to informing him of his daughter's birth, consented to its use as a frontispiece:

> Dear Lahr, Enclosed you will find two dozen copies of drawings signed by me. Glad you are printing *Darkness* in the *New Coterie*, and I am sure I'll be delighted to have you put the drawing as a frontispiece. I like it very much and so do my friends. I think it is frightfully good (Kelly 1996, 147).

Darkness: A Tragedy in Three Acts appeared in the third issue of *The New Coterie* (Summer 1926, 42–68) with a portrait by Roberts. Subsequently, E. Archer, based at 68 Red Lion Sq, London, published 112 copies in May 1926: 12 to meet copyright requirements and 100 – signed and numbered by the author for sale, also with a frontispiece by Roberts.[24]

William O'Flaherty
William Roberts' 1926 sketch of Liam O'Flaherty
used as frontispiece for *Darkness: A Tragedy in Three Acts*

Lahr, as requested, arranged for a private reading to establish performance copyright. The event occurred at William Roberts' art studio[25] Chalk Farm, near Camden Town, north of London, on 27 April 1926, and the cast consisted of R. Dornan[26] (Mary), K.S. Bhat (Dark Daniel), Mrs. Sarah Roberts[27] (Beautiful Bridget), Marthe Goldberg (Proud Margaret), and Rhys Davies[28] (Merry Brian).

Rhys Davies (1901–1978)

The artist in question was William Roberts, husband of Sarah Kramer Roberts, who played Brigit/Bridget in the reading. Roberts, whose paintings and style are '... sly and sardonic in observation, his tubular, inflated or exaggeratedly angular figures peopling a world of heraldic colour and rigid geometry' (Shone 1992, 394), provided art for several of Lahr's publications.[29]

Sarah and William Roberts (Paris 1924)

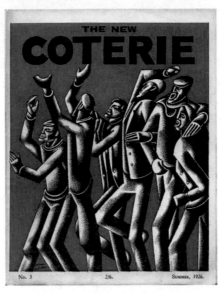

The New Coterie (Summer 1926), in which *Darkness* appeared.
Cover by William Roberts

'Taking the Oath', William Roberts' 1920 depiction of Irish
politicians swearing the controversial Oath of Allegiance
with a map of a partitioned Ireland in the background

Ireland had changed considerably since O'Flaherty's student days and even since his brief reign in the Rotunda:

> Dublin had changed too. The Civil War was over and the country had settled down to the business of making a nation out of the shambles of rebellion and war. The writers set themselves to the job of deciding their roles and the role of literature in the new nation (Zimmer 1970, 1).

The early years of the Irish Free State represented a high point for Irish-language drama in terms of visibility and the number of productions in the capital city. With the aid of a 1924 government subsidy from Minister Ernest Blythe, An Comhar Drámaíochta established a stable financial base.

Founded the previous year from the remnants of several pre-War of Independence amateur theatrical groups – Na hAisteoirí in particular, and frequently referred to by that designation (O'Leary 2004, 465) – An Comhar Drámaíochta, like An Gúm, was charged with promoting, cultivating, and popularizing Irish-language culture. While An Gúm's brief concerned commissioning, translating, and publishing textbooks and literary books for the entire state, An Comhar Drámaíochta's assignment pertained to the production and staging of original and translated plays in Irish in the city of Dublin only. In contrast to state subvention of Irish-language publishing, support for Irish-language theatre helped create a popular, communal, public, urban-based spectacle. It offered not only a visual and visible Irish-language cultural activity but also created an Irish-language acoustic (Ó Tuathaigh 2008, 26–48) in the metropolitan centre that simply could not be achieved through the solitary and private act of reading. In tandem with the state subsidy,

Gearóid Ó Lochlainn's return to Ireland from Denmark added theatrical expertise, experience, and a European élan to an established, albeit informal and loose, amateur acting structure in Irish-language circles (Ó Siadhail 1993, 58).

Among those involved in An Comhar Drámaíochta was León Ó Broin,

> a highly cultured and deeply conservative man ... who served as editor of *Maria Legionis*, the organ of Frank Duff's Legion of Mary, but also (as) a man interested in encouraging dialogue among religious, cultural and political groups ... (Savage 2010, 8).

Ó Broin recounted in his memoir how drama provided citizens, specifically civil servants such as him, an opportunity to engage in Irish-language activity without endorsing or participating in the language movement's increasingly fractious and divisive politics. As the earlier enthusiasm and energy associated with the language revival waned, state initiatives attempted to fill the void left by declining popular demand. Conradh na Gaeilge/Gaelic League and its newspaper *Fáinne an Lae*, under the editorship of the brilliant but bellicose Ó Grianna, targeted the Cumann na nGaedheal government and their (in)activity with respect to reviving and promoting Irish (O'Leary 2004, 23–89; Mac Congáil 2003, iv–xix). In his memoir, Ó Broin recalled how the language movement lost lustre:

> (B)y 1925 the edge had gone off some of the earlier enthusiasm. I had seen in the Central Branch of the Gaelic League and in the Leinster College of Irish the crowds of teachers, civil servants and others that flocked to learn the language in 1922, but the beginnings of a decline of interest had set in as a result of the civil war and through the discovery that Irish was a difficult language to learn (Ó Broin n.d., 67).

A couple of pages later, he noted:

> I was by now inclined to dissociate myself from the
> Gaelic League, which was just as well perhaps as the
> Department of Education and its officials had become
> cock-shots in the League's paper. I was tiring of the
> political atmosphere of the Executive Committee of
> which I had been elected a member and was giving more
> of my time to the production of plays in Irish by a Gaelic
> Drama League of which I was secretary ... (Ó Broin n.d.,
> 69).

An Comhar Drámaíochta, with an office located at
122A St Stephen's Green (the same address as the
Folklore Commission), performed plays, both Irish-
language originals and translated texts, two nights per
month and a Sunday matinee, when possible, from
October to April (O'Leary 2004, 465) on the Abbey
Theatre stage. During the 1925–1926 season, it
performed 37 plays, 16 of which were new plays and
four of which were subsequently published (Ó
Súilleabháin 1972, 3).[30] The notion of attracting urban
audiences, comprised of well-disposed learners and
proficient speakers, to attend predominately
entertaining, light-hearted, humorous shows in the
capital had obvious merit, but the festering resentment
bred by the Civil War and its atrocities, neither
forgotten nor forgiven, was a major and unconsidered
factor. While there was no direct link between the Civil
War and An Comhar Drámaíochta, the composition of
the troupe's executive committee and the key roles of
prominent individuals – Piaras Béaslaí, former military
censor, and León Ó Broin, former Free State army
officer – convinced republicans that it was pro-treaty in
ideology and praxis. This led to the belief that it was
certainly unwelcoming to those who had, and in
principle still, opposed the Treaty.

Piaras Béalsaí (1881–1965)

'Boundaries between politics and culture in the first years of the Free State were', as Allen correctly observes, 'fluid'. 'Political organizations, government and opposition, involved themselves in art, their members attending theatres and galleries, keeping diaries, writing memoirs' (Allen 2009, 46). For many republicans, An Comhar Drámaíochta was a Free State guild: 'Is dealraitheach gur creideadh gur lucht tacaíochta de chuid an tSaorstáit ba mhó a bhí le fáil ann' (Ó Siadhail 1993, 60–61). ('It appears that it was believed to be mainly the preserve of those who supported the Free State'). In a linguistic and cultural setting where drama was seen as a medium to teach the state-sanctioned linguistic vernacular to actors and audience members alike and to inspire laughter, patriotism, and national identity (Ní Mhuircheartaigh & Mac Congáil 2008, 27, 7–33), *Dorchadas* was hardly standard fare.

Dublin theatre-goers, recovered from the excitement and furor that greeted the Abbey's production of Sean O'Casey's *The Plough and the Stars*[31] (8–13 February) and having feasted on Jules Romains' *Doctor Knock* translated by Harley Granville-Barker (16–20 February) and Oliver Goldsmith's *She Stoops to Conqueror* (22–27 February), were spoiled for choice in early March 1926. The Abbey offered George Shiels' three-act comedy *Professor Tim* from 2–6 March. Following *Professor Tim* were three plays from 8–13 March: *In the Zone* by Eugene O'Neill, *Deirdre* by W.B. Yeats, and *Damer's Gold* by Lady Gregory. In addition, the Republican Players, under the auspices of Cumann na mBan, staged three more plays at the Abbey on Sunday 7 March:

> One of them, *Lustre*, is by the late Seamus O'Kelly, now produced in Dublin for the first time. *Meadowsweet*, by the same author, has already proved popular with Dublin audiences, and *Lustre* promises to be equally successful. The other works in the programme are *The Lad from Largymore*, by Seamus MacManus; and *Eilis agus an Bhean Deirce*,[32] by 'Cú Uladh.' Musical selections by the Clann Lir orchestra will be given during the intervals (M.A.T., *The Sunday Independent* 7 March 1926, 2).

The *Irish Independent*'s Monday edition (1 March 1926, 6) featured an advertisement, giving prominence to *Dorchadas*, stating a starting time of 8:00 p.m. and an array of admission prices: 5/9, 3/6, 3/-, 2/-, 1/6, and 1/3.

Previously *The Sunday Independent* announced on 28 February that An Comhar Drámaíochta would perform two Irish-language plays the following Monday on the Abbey Theatre stage: Liam O'Flaherty's *Dorchadas* and Fiachra Éilgeach's (Ristéard Ó Foghludha, 1871–1957) *Ag Suirghe leis an mBaintrigh*.[33] The report explained that this announcement differed from the advertised schedule:

> *Ar Ealodh*, the adaption by Leon Ó Broin of a modern French comedy, which was originally announced for production to-morrow, has had to be postponed owing to

the illness of one of the principals. Mr. Liam O'Flaherty, author of *Dorchadas*, is a widely-known novelist, and his new work will be found to be an intensely realistic study which should add enormously to the high artistic reputation of An Comhar Dramuiochta (*Sunday Independent* 28 February 1926, 2).

ABBEY THEATRE

ᴠɪᴀ Luain, Laó maᴚᴛa, 8 p.m.

na h-aisteóirí

ᴠoᴚċaᴅas (Liam Ó Flaitⱱeaⱱeaⱱⱨ).

as sⱳⱨⱨe leis an mⱱaⱳⱨⱨⱨⱨ
(Fracⱨa Citgeaċ).

ᴠⱨⱨ Isⱨeac ...... 5/9, 3/6, 3/-, 2/-, 1/6, 1/3.

Advertisement for *Dorchadas* at the Abbey Theatre.
An Comhar Drámaíochta was frequently referred to as *Na hAisteoirí*, an earlier dramatic troupe.

Gearóid Ó Lochlainn directed the following cast of Na hAisteoirí/An Comhar Drámaíochta actors: Máire Ní Chinnéide[34] (Brighid Bhreágh), Máire Ní Oisín[35] (Maighreád Uaibhreach), Máire Ní Shíothcháin/Ní Shíocháin[36] (Máire Mhór), and Muiris Ó Catháin[37] (Domhnall Dorcha). Ó Lochlainn played the part of Brian Gealgháireach himself.

Ó Broin remembered the production in his memoir:

(T)he dramatics were both on the stage and off it. We were told that some university students intended to prevent the play being done at all, as had been attempted before with Synge's *Playboy* and O'Casey's *Plough and the Stars*. I went to General Murphy[38], the Deputy Commissioner of the Garda whom I had got to know in the army, and he filled the house and wings with plain-clothes men on the night. There was no disturbance whatsoever, however, which I rather regretted, for there is nothing like a row to publicise a play (Ó Broin n.d., 70).

An Comhar Drámaíochta, 1923
from left: (seated): Proinnsias Ní Chruadhlaoich, Piaras Béaslaí, Máire Ní Chinnéide, Fiachra Éilgeach, Máire Ní Oisín *(standing)*: Tadhg Ó Scanaill, Micheál Ó Siochfhradha; Pádraig Ó Broithe, Niamh Nic Ghearailt, Gearóid Ó Lochlainn, Nóra Ní Chathasaigh, Amhlaibh Mac Aindrias, Séamas Ó Scanaill, Muiris Ó Cathain

A year earlier, on 12 March, the same General Murphy, as commissioner of the Dublin civic guard, had assisted Frank Duff's effort to close the notorious Monto section in Dublin north inner city, namely the area around Connolly Station from Montogmery Street and Foley Street to the Liffey. Monto was regarded as one of the largest red light districts in Europe, and Duff (1889–1980) – founder of the Legion of Mary, which was established in 1921 as a lay apostolic organization at the service of the Catholic Church and under its guidance – and the Jesuit R.S. Devane campaigned to shut down permanently the numerous brothels. On 12 March 1925, during Lent, with Garda support supplied by Murphy, Duff and his supporters succeeded in bringing the district's primary business to a halt, nailing crucifixes on the doors and securing 120 arrests.[39]

Despite a full house on both nights, the lack of compensation for his work irked O'Flaherty, who alluded to this point in the *Irish Statesman* when he clashed with Úna Dix (Uí Dhíosca) (1880–1958) over his decision to write in English rather than exclusively in Irish.[40]

The play not only attracted full houses but also received several reviews in national newspapers in both languages:

> On Monday night the Gaelic Players played two plays before a full house. The first was a three-act tragedy by Liam O'Flaherty which is rightly entitled *Gloom* ... The actors must be excused, for the play was produced at extremely short notice, but Máire · Ní Shíocháin, who played the rather thankless part of the mother, could greatly improve her part if she allowed herself more crescendo instead of becoming fortissimo immediately. Muiris Ó Catháin and Gearóid Ó Lochlainn, who played the parts of Dan and Brian, deserve great praise. The second play, a slight comedy, *Flirting with the Widow*,[41] was extremely well played by all the cast, notably Máire Ní Oisín and Máire Ní Shíocháin (*Irish Statesman* 1926, 802).

Máire Ní Shíocháin's pitch drew adverse comment from 'Eoin' in the *Irish Independent*, who conceded that the play was good but would benefit from less crying and wailing. The old woman, the reviewer complained, was excessive with her voice and actions when cursing the world around her (*Irish Independent* 3 March 1926, 8).

The Irish Times reviewer was also critical of Ní Shíocháin's voice, though not as harsh:

> Máire Ní Shíocháin made the mistake of beginning on too high a note, leaving herself no reserves; but she was impressive. As the girl's mother, Máire Ní Chinnéide was exceedingly good – sympathetic, and even majestic – Máire Ní Oisín was not too well cast for the girl's part which needed subtler treatment of emotion (*Irish Times* 2 March 1926, 5).

Such faults, however, were not uncommon and often resulted from the lack of opportunities to correct them, as 'Aodh Éigeas' explained in *The Leader* (July 1926):

> The Irish players have been on for only one night a month. That means that the players have only a 'first night' of every play they stage after all their trouble, and with no chance of correcting inevitable slips of dialogue, etc. first nights reveal (O'Leary 2004, 473).

Another mitigating factor was, as Ó Broin complained, Ó Lochlainn's penchant for acting in plays which he also directed:

> The repertoire, even with translations, was slim; that there could only be one performance a month meant that the audience effectively saw only a dress rehearsal; and Ó Lochlainn made a cardinal mistake in being both producer and actor … (Ó Broin n.d., 69).

Further, not only was the production produced in haste due to the cancellation of *Ar Ealodh*, but Máire Ní Oisín and Muiris Ó Scanail performed in both plays on both nights, as the *Irish Times* critic discerned.[42]

The reviewers did not limit their comments to the production or the acting but offered interpretations of the play and its motivations. The *Irish Times* was the most generous in its praise:

> It proved to be exceedingly interesting and it was somewhat surprising to find a novelist proving himself

so well skilled in stagecraft: for the play was wholly free from amateur weakness … It was finely staged last night. The characters in the romantic Western fisherfolk's attire familiarised by Synge's plays, were vivid and convincing, and their language had a native eloquence, more satisfying than Synge's unreal diction … The play is immeasurably better than any of the author's novels and quite the most ambitious thing done by the Gaelic Players (*Irish Times* 2 March 1926, 5).

The chief criticism was *Dorchadas'* similarity to *Birthright*, a drama by the Cork realist T. C. Murray (1873–1959); according to the *Irish Times*, '… it has a closely similar theme – jealousy among brothers, issuing in tragedy' (2 March 1926, 5).[43] First produced by the Abbey in 1910, *Birthright* appeared there at least once per year every year from 1910–1932 (with the exception of four years: 1921, 1924, 1925, and 1926). Given *Dorchadas'* theme and social discourse, it is not difficult to link it also with Pádraic Ó Conaire's *Bairbre Rua*, which was published by the Gaelic League/ Conradh na Gaeilge (1908) and earned the £15 Oireachtas dramatic prize the same year (Ní Chionnaith 1995, 134–35; Riggs 1994, 34–35).

While endorsing the display's potential, 'Oscar Óg', the *Irish Statesman*'s reviewer, was less enthusiastic about the structure of *Dorchadas*:

Though the play may be faulty in many ways, yet it is encouraging to find original work of such promise being done … The play has two faults: firstly, there is a feeling that too much has been done in a short space, it needs and could bear elaboration, and, secondly, it lacks dignity, especially in the third act. Here it is dangerously near melodrama, and needs more careful treatment not to be even funny in parts (*Irish Statesman* 6 March 1926, 802).

In keeping with the divided nature of Irish society in the post-Civil War setting, *Fáinne an Lae*, Conradh na Gaeilge/The Gaelic League's weekly newspaper, attempted to serve two masters and offered its readers two reviews on the same page. 'Neol'[44] (*Fáinne an Lae* 13 March 1926, 2), lauded the play as a work with an artistic style and continuity that flowed in one terrifying crescendo from beginning to end. The review argued that Irish-language literature would benefit from similar plays. If the audience found it too dark or depressing, that was a consequence of their lack of familiarity with its modern style, with which they would become more acquainted in the future. This reference to a new style, as distinct perhaps from the Abbey Theatre's standard trope of peasant plays and cottage-realism, may refer to the characters' emotional intensity and Ó Lochlainn's use of light and sound effects during the production. However, it also echoes the Dublin Drama's League's

> interest in continental theatrical experiments in 'new psychological exploration' which, in turn, encouraged innovations in staging, lighting, acting and movement to reflect new forms of writing for the theatre (Sisson 2010, 133).

Two years later in October 1928, Ó Lochlainn would combine with Mac Liammóir and Edwards to produce The Gate Theatre Studio. As Sisson writes:

> By the early 1930s, the Gate Studio Theatre finished its relationship with the Peacock, and moved to its present location at the Rotunda to become the Gate Theatre. During some of the most turbulent years of the emergence and foundation of the State, the Dublin Drama League, the Peacock Theatre and the Gate were determined to introduce and promote experimental voices as part of their education as artists and performers, but also as a bulwark against conservatism and increasing cultural isolationism (Sisson 2010, 144).

One might argue that in Ó Lochlainn's production of *Dorchadas*, that sense of experimentation and audacity that would flower later is already present. As for 'Neol', he concluded his review by universally praising the cast but singling out Muiris Ó Cathain for special recognition.

On the same page, directly beneath Neol's 'An Dorchadas', appeared '*Dorchadas* – Tuairim Eile' (*Dorchadas* – Another Opinion) by 'Theo', a resoundingly unflattering review. In typical fashion the first blow was to question the quality and purity of the Irish in use, followed by the relevance of the entire second act. Rejecting the notion that the play accurately depicted the Aran islanders, 'Theo' assigned the play's evildoings and corrupt thoughts instead to the playwright's own mind, openly asking if a decent Irish-language playwright who was also a Christian existed given the play's depravity. S/he attributed such degeneracy to the Russian literary influence on the author rather than the people of Aran. *Dorchadas*, it was argued, is another *Playboy*, O'Flaherty another Synge. The play failed to satisfy Aristotle's criteria for drama, lacking not only *katharsis* (sic) but *une douce terreur et une pitié charmanta*, as well. 'Theo' concluded by noting that if the reviewer sought such plays, s/he knew they could be found at the Queen's, where at least the authors did not pretend the villains were from the *Gaeltacht*.

'Splannc', writing in *An Sguab*, a Galway-based newspaper from 1922–1926, considered all four reviewers s/he had read to be misguided. *Dorchadas*, in her/his opinion, was an allegory on recent Irish political history. The brothers, arguing over the girl, represented the Free Staters and Republicans, making fools of themselves by killing one another over Cáit Ní

Ghaidhir, who remains a pathetic wreck. The two old women, 'Splannc' believed, represented the Old Irish – those who would sell a son or a daughter in order to secure peace for themselves. If this thesis proved true, 'Splannc' argued, the author's message was that the Irish people deserved their pathetic end. S/he concluded the letter by praising the author and urging the play's intended audience to read and reread it (*An Sguab*, April 1926, 64).

Full houses and national media attention notwithstanding, 'Splannc's' assessment signaled something of an end of conversation about *Dorchadas*, as reviews petered out. The play did not become part of An Comhar Drámaíochta's standard repertoire, and little else was heard of it as a stage production.

There would, however, be another twist in the multicultural saga that is *Dorchadas*, although it appears that this penultimate act was played out unbeknownst to O'Flaherty. In 1929 An Comhar Drámaíochta submitted a series of dramatic scripts to An Gúm for consideration, *Dorchadas* among them.[45] An Gúm, founded in 1926, was another nation-building project established for promoting Irish-language publishing and included textbooks, original Irish writing – fiction and non-fiction – and translations.[46] In accordance with standard policy, each text was sent to two external reviewers for written review, with *Dorchadas* going to Piaras Béaslaí and Daniel Corkery on 16 October 1929. Béaslaí returned a blunt, but positive, one-line appraisal on November 14: 'Dráma bríoghmar é seo agus is dóich liom gur cheart é d'fhoillsiú'. ('This is a lively play and I believe it should be published') (An Gúm 233/221).

Daniel Corkery (1878–1964)

Corkery's review was more detailed and considered:

Meoldráma é seo agus mar le meolodráma tá sé go maith. Tá cúpla bliain ann ó scríobh an t-úghdhar é agus b'fhéidir go bhféadfadh sé é fheabhsú anois dá mba mhaith leis é athscríobadh. Cuid de, ba dhóigh le duine gur gharsún ocht bliana deug d'aois do scríobh, tá an oiread san fiántais ann. Ba cheart seans do thabhairt do Liam smacht do chur ar an sgéal anois. Tá abairt annso is annsúd nar cheart iad do chur i gcló.

(This is a melodrama and as a melodrama it is good. It is a few years since the author wrote it and maybe he could control it better if he wished to rewrite it. Parts appear to be written by an eighteen-year old such is the ferocity. Liam should be given an opportunity to improve the story now. There is the occasional sentence that should not be published).

On 27 November 1929, Seán Mac Lelland, An Gúm's chief publications' officer, sent an English-language letter to the Deputy Secretary informing him:

This is a play in Irish by Liam O'Flaherty. It was produced by the Comhar some time ago, and the script was forwarded to me by the Secretary of the Comhar with a number of other plays. The Committee recommended its acceptance for publication under the General Literature Scheme, but they think the author should be given an opportunity of revising the text first. Before taking any action on the matter I should like you to give consideration to the point whether it is proper to publish under our Scheme works by authors such as O'Flaherty, who, if he wished to publish a play in Irish, would have no difficulty in getting an ordinary publisher to take the risk (An Gúm 233/221).

Two days later, the secretary received another note from Mac Lelland, titled 'Publication of Play by Liam O'Flaherty':

Secretary, Leaving aside for the moment all other considerations and objections, I consider that there is no proper process or application before us for making this publication. I don't know what right or authority the Sec. of the Comhar had to offer the work for publication, but I can hazard a guess as to what the author would say and do if we published it. I recommend no further action (An Gúm 233/221).

A handwritten note at the bottom of the page indicated that the manuscript was returned to An Comhar Drámaíochta.

Given Corkery's previous close relationship with Frank O'Connor – his former pupil and protégé – it seems possible that they might have discussed this episode and that it may have informed O'Connor's opinion in his 1934 article 'Two Languages' in *The Bookman*:[47]

You can keep a language from decaying but you cannot make it live. Irish is being kept in existence to-day simply because the Government attaches certain penalties to ignorance of it, and makes it a profitable matter for those who can use it. It maintains a publishing concern solely for the purpose of distributing books in Irish. In Dublin you may see a new bookshop with a very fine display of books in coloured jackets, and at prices as reasonable as those charged for similar books in English. If you look over them you will probably discover that the authors' names are familiar: here are Freeman Wills Crofts, Helen Mathers, Lew Wallace, Joseph Conrad, Ridgwell Cullum, Rider Haggard, George Birmingham, Bram Stoker, Dickens, Emily Brontë, Goldsmith, Frank Packard, Captain Marryat and Wilkie Collins. You will not find the names of Seán O Faoláin, Peadar O'Donnell or Liam O'Flaherty. I may be prejudiced, but it seems to me that there is something unnatural about this. Out of the hundreds of thousands of pounds which are being spent upon Irish, there is quite a comfortable living to be made by original writers, and Liam O'Flaherty's Irish is very fine, while Seán O Faoláin's stories were written originally in Irish. Besides there is the danger that translation may have exactly the opposite effect to that intended by Gaels. Instead of being satisfied with the half-dozen or so detective stories provided for his benefit, the book-shy Irish-speaker may conceive a passion for them and go on to read them in English. Even Government seems to be aware of this danger, because handsome prizes are offered for original work in Irish. Yet the books are not forthcoming. Very strange, you say (O'Donovan 1934, 240).

Nor is this article alone in highlighting O'Flaherty's glaring omission from An Gúm's stable of authors and translators. An unnamed correspondent writing in *The Saturday Review* in 1930 connected O'Flaherty, the recently established Board of Censors, and An Gúm as follows:

In view of the fact that Irish is one of the official languages of this country, it seems strange that the Gaelic League is not represented on the Board of Censors. The omission, however, may be deliberate and intended to indicate that our truly native productions can be trusted never to offend purity; and, in the agitations for a censorship, stress was laid almost wholly on imported publications. All our own well-known writers, other than those whose medium is Irish – from Mr. W.B. Yeats to Mr. Liam O'Flaherty – have London publishers; and their works, therefore, come under the heading of imported publications. It is interesting in this connection to note that Irish publishing becomes more and more dependent on the issue of works in the Irish language. These are now of all sorts; writers of Irish no longer confine themselves to moralistic tracts and propaganda for the old tongue. The propagandist notion creeps in, however, in the attempt to popularize Irish lessons by providing the public with translations of popular 'foreign' fiction. The Gaelic League now includes in its members experts in detective stories. One of these, after trying his own hand in this form of literature, has recently translated A.E.W. Mason's *At the Villa Rose* onto Irish; and another English book that has been brought before the Gaelic public is R.L. Stevenson's *Dr. Jekyll and Mr. Hyde*. It must be remembered that the mentality of the average Irish Gaelic Leaguer is far removed from that of the Western islanders; and it is the mentality of the Gaelic League which commands at present the development of modern Ireland. Our Gaelic intellectuals suppose that a national literature expresses a so-called national thought; and this leads to provincialism. Benedetto Croce's advice to young Italy would be useful here: To feel nationally, but to think like cosmopolitans (*Saturday Review* 8 March 1930, 290).

Several years before An Gúm rejected *Dorchadas*, O'Flaherty's burgeoning reputation as a novelist and short story writer was such that collectors had already begun to take an interest in acquiring his manuscripts. Among them was Percy H. Muir (1894–1979), an agent for Dulau & Co., who wrote to O'Flaherty inquiring if he had manuscripts for sale. O'Flaherty responded on 3 July 1926, that he was wiling to sell the manuscript of *Darkness* and *Dorchadas*:

> Dear Mr Muir, I have also the MS of a three-act play *Darkness* which I would be willing to sell for fifteen pounds. It is written in Gaelic originally by me. I afterwards translated it into English. The Gaelic MS would be, of course, merely a curiosity for your client (Kelly 1996, 155–56).

It is unclear if Muir purchased either text, but O'Flaherty boasted in the *Irish Statesman* (December 1927) that he sold the Irish-language manuscript to an English socialist:

> Although the theatre was packed, which rarely happens for these Gaelic plays, I was never paid for the production. Here is the joke. The only remuneration I received for this play was from an English socialist who dislikes Irish and everything connected with nationalism of any sort in any place. He paid me twenty five pounds for the Gaelic manuscript, i.e. for my handwriting (*Irish Statesman* 1927, 348)[48]

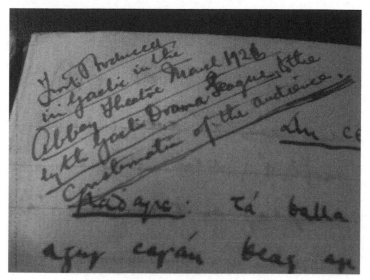

'First produced in Gaelic in the Abbey Theatre March 1926 by the Gaelic Drama League to the consternation of the audience' – O'Flaherty's reference to the Abbey production on the Kentucky manuscript

Currently, the Department of Special Collections at the University of Kentucky's Margaret I. King Library holds two handwritten O'Flaherty manuscripts: the complete manuscript of *Dorchadas* and a draft of the play's second and third acts. The complete manuscript has a handwritten note: 'First produced in Gaelic in the Abbey Theatre March 1926 by the Gaelic Drama League to the consternation of the audience'. It is unclear when the manuscripts, acquired for $150, came to the University of Kentucky. In addition, the James Hardiman Library at the National University of Ireland, Galway is in possession of a typescript of *Dorchadas* with handwritten stage directions, which apparently was used by a production or cast member. The English-language script copy used by Rhys Davies for the production in the Roberts' studio resides in Special Collections at the Boston Public Library in Boston, Massachusetts.[49]

By the 1930s the Irish Censorship Board took aim at O'Flaherty's books with increasing frequency, banning *The House of Gold* in 1930, *The Puritan* in 1931, and *The Martyr* in 1933. With the dissolution of his relationship with Margaret Barrington-O'Flaherty in March 1931, he faded from the public scene and 'except for the records of publication of his books and stories not much is available about O'Flaherty's personal life from 1927 to 1932' (Zimmer 1970, 32).

1934 found him living on Sunset Boulevard in Los Angeles, working for Paramount Pictures and hoping to find success at script writing. Whether O'Flaherty was aware of efforts to publish his work with An Gúm remains unclear. But on returning to Ireland in 1946, he revealed in an interview with the *Irish Press* that:

> (O)ne of the first things I did here was to tour the Gúm and the bookshops. I was surprised, after what I had read, to find excellent works by writers of Irish. I renewed acquaintance with books by the older hands like Mac Grianna, but also I was delighted to find new writers and new books. There was a first-class work by a new writer named Ó Cadhain and there were fine stories by Tomas Bairéad. Then I came across a charming book about wanderings in Mayo. I forget its name and the name of its author, but in the middle of it I found an old song I sang in Aran as a child and it brought back many memories (O'Flaherty 13 May 1946, 4).

Among other comments – some in jest, some provocative – O'Flaherty talked about *Dorchadas*, the interviewer describing that part of their conversation thusly:

> He is enthusiastic about the idea of a Gaelic theatre. He recalled that himself and Pádraic Ó Conaire once set out

to establish a touring Gaelic theatre. O'Flaherty wrote a play for it, *Dorchadas* (Darkness) but the theatre was never born. 'At the time there was too much narrow prejudice against it', he said 'and also we had the very patriotic Cosgrave Government' (O'Flaherty 13 May 1946, 4).

Máirtín Ó Cadhain (1906–1970)

In 1953, the same year that Sairséal agus Dill published *Dúil*, his only Irish-language short story collection, *Darkness* resurfaced in an unusual and unexpected forum. Having returned to writing in Irish under the guidance of his nephew Breandán Ó hEithir, O'Flaherty revisited his Irish-language stories from the 1920s to prepare them for publication. He may have pondered publishing *Dorchadas* in Irish, but the manuscripts were gone. However, the translation published by Lahr was available, and it appeared in *American Aphrodite: A Quarterly for the Fancy Free*, a risqué American journal edited by the notorious Samuel Roth, aka 'the Pirate Roth'.

Born in 1893, Samuel Roth was an American Jewish writer and publisher who achieved notoriety in 1922 for publishing an unauthorized version of *Ulysses* that led to a protest by James Joyce and a jail sentence for Roth when he was prosecuted for publishing obscene material. Released and undeterred, he also published portions of *Finnegans Wake*, again without permission, in *Two World's Quarterly* as well as unauthorized versions of work by D.H. Lawrence and Thomas Hardy. The first issue of *American Aphrodite: A Quarterly for the Fancy Free* appeared in 1951 and listed Roth as editor with two Monaghan men as co-editors: Peter and Patrick Kavanagh. Peter, who had come to the United States in 1946 to teach in Brooklyn, New York, recalled in his memoir how in 1951, Milton Hindus facilitated a meeting with Roth where the American invited Kavanagh to write for a new journal, *American Aphrodite*. Kavanagh knew little of Roth except the notorious printing of Joyce's text:

American Aphrodite, Vol. 3, No. 11, 1953

When I visited Roth at his office I found him to be a tall fellow wearing spectacles, unusually courteous, almost courtly. He quickly ordered up tea. After talking to me for a few minutes it must have been clear to him that he had an innocent on his hands. I brought forward Patrick's name. He knew Patrick, liked his work and immediately wrote out a cheque for $100.00 made out to him as an advance on a piece of writing that I promised I would have him send. I mailed the cheque to Patrick who after receiving it had high praise for me as a literary agent (Kavanagh 2000, 248).

Patrick Kavanagh acknowledged receipt of Roth's check in a letter to Peter dated 12 March 1951, sent from 62 Pembroke Road, Dublin (Kavanagh 1969, 161–2). The brothers' relationship with Roth, however, soon took a peculiar and unsettling turn. 'When some months later (1951) the magazine appeared there on the cover as co-editors was my name and that of Patrick. This didn't make sense' (Kavanagh 2000, 248).

Peter's shock had less to do with the cover than the contents. In addition to Patrick's poem 'Jungle' and 'The Sighing Age' by Sean O'Faolain:

(A)bout one-third of the magazine was devoted to what then was considered pornography. Today it would hardly merit the title of soft porn but in those early years the law was very strict on what was considered obscene. As editor I could be charged with pornography, put in jail, deported (Kavanagh 2000, 248).

Peter wrote to Patrick requesting his assistance in distancing the two of them from the publication. Ironically, in light of what would transpire with the collapse of *Kavanagh's Weekly* and his calamitous decision to sue *The Leader* for libel in October 1952 (Walsh 2010), Patrick, who had already cashed the check, 'thought the incident a great joke', treating Peter's 'concern as if (sic) were of no interest to him'. (Kavanagh 2000, 248) A lawyer with political connections acted on Peter's behalf and cleared him of any responsibility for the contents of the magazine; the Kavanaghs' names appeared on no further issues of *American Aphrodite*. Nonetheless Peter would recall Roth as 'an amusing rascal and not without a literary flair' (Kavanagh 1977, 139–40).

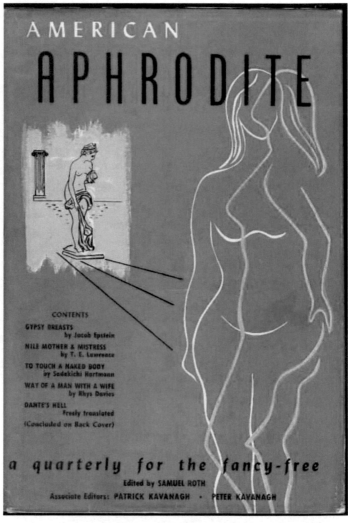

American Aphrodite, Vol. 1, No. 1, 1951
Associate Editors, Patrick Kavanagh and Peter Kavanagh

The authorities in the United States cared less for literary flair. At this stage Roth ran a mail-order service centred in New York, and many of the books he sold were remainder stock, small cheap paperbacks, and 'flip-through' nudie books in which women seemed to undress. In 1955, a Senate subcommittee investigating pornography's impact on youth crime ordered him to appear. He did and taunted senators by suggesting they take an intelligence and literacy test before accusing him of pornography. It is hardly surprising, then, that in 1956:

> (H)e was sentenced under federal law to five years in prison and fined $5000 for selling through the mail his magazine *American Aphrodite*, books of female nudes, and an edition of Aubrey Beardsley's illustrated *The Story of Venus and TannhŠuser*. The mix of materials were pure Roth – *American Aphrodite* usually featured things like mild erotic line drawings, some piece of long-out-of-print British literature (the 'scandalous' 17th-century plays of Aphra Behn appear in many issues), a 'bawdy' new translation from Chaucer, and something truly shocking, like nude photos of 10-year-old girls taken in Victorian brothels (Bronski 2002).

As he had with previous guilty verdicts, Roth appealed, and the case went all the way to the United States Supreme Court. In a landmark 6–3 decision, the court ruled on 24 June 1957, that while the First Amendment to the US Constitution protected art, literature, and scientific research, even if they had sexual content, obscene material was not protected. Obscenity, the court declared, had to be 'utterly without redeeming social importance', a ruling that changed the US legal system's view of censorship. On this distinction, however, Roth served another five years in prison.

Before the authorities intervened, Roth and a series of co-editors published 20 issues of *American Aphrodite* in five volumes – four numbers per year between 1951 and 1955. The magazine featured stories and poems by Sean O'Faolain, Frank O'Connor, Anais Nin, Ernest Gebler, T.F. Powys, D.H. Lawrence, Roy Campell, Rhys Davies, David Garnett, LAG Strong, Patrick Reardon Conner, and Richard Aldington, among others. O'Flaherty was included in the second issue, which featured 'Unclean', and as late as Volume 5 (1955), when 'The Touch', a translation of his 'Teagmháil', appeared in the magazine's penultimate number. 'Unclean', a story previously published in *The Wild Swan and Other Stories* (1932) and set in Dublin's Monto, tells of a rural married merchant coming to Dublin to collect rent from his tenants, one of whom is clearly managing a brothel. Seduced by a pretty prostitute who subsequently robs him, he is arrested and spends a night in a cell declaring himself unclean. As for 'The Touch', positioning it in such a journal with accompanying illustrations places a greater emphasis on certain aspects of the text than a reader appreciates when reading it in *Dúil*.

Darkness appeared in *American Aphrodite: A Quarterly for the Fancy Free*, Vol. 3, no. 11 (1953), with the entire issue dedicated to O'Flaherty's work, although no mention is made of him in the introduction. The volume's theme appears to be censorship, as many of the featured texts were previously censored, but again, no specific reference is made to the history of *Darkness* or O'Flaherty's relationships with An Gúm and the Irish Censorship Board.

Conclusion

Breandán Ó hEithir concluded his informative essay about his uncle with an admonishment for would-be critics of O'Flaherty's decision to write primarily in English:

> Tá sé fánach a bheith ag tomhais anois cén toradh a bheadh ar shaothar Uí Fhlatharta dá bhfanadh sé i mbun scríbhneoireachta i nGaeilge ó lár na bhficheadaí i leith agus dá gcaithfeadh sé tréimhsí ní b'fhaide sa Ghaeltacht. Ní mheasaim go bhfuil ciall le bheith ag tuairimíocht mar go bhfuilim cinnte gur theastaigh ón bhFlaithartach cloí le scríbhneoireacht mar ghléas beatha ó tháinig sé faoi thionchar Edward Garnett i 1923 agus ó foilsíodh *Thy Neighbour's Wife* an bhliain chéanna. Tá mé lánchinnte freisin go mbeadh sé thar a bheith sásta a bheith ina scríbhneoir lánaimseartha Gaeilge dá mb'fhéidir é, ach is róléir nach raibh ansin ach brionglóid cé go ndeachaigh oidhe Uí Chonaire go mór i gcion air agus gur shocraigh sé a bheith neamhspleách – chomh fada agus is féidir d'aon scríbhneoir a bheith neamhspleách (Ó hEithir 1977, 76).

(It is pointless to guess what direction O'Flaherty's work would have taken had he persisted with writing in Irish from the mid-twenties onward and had he spent longer periods in the Irish-speaking area. I don't think such reasoning is sensible because I'm certain that Liam wanted to survive on his writing once he came under Edward Garnett's influence in 1923 and once *Thy Neighbour's Wife* was published the same year. I am also fully certain that he would have been satisfied to have been a fulltime Irish language author had that been possible, but it is clear that that was only a dream though the tragedy of Ó Conaire made an impression on him and he decided to be independent – in as far as any writer can be independent).

It may indeed be idle speculation to wonder what might have happened had O'Flaherty continued writing in Irish or had he spent more time in the *Gaeltacht*. Equally, there is no reason to question either

Ó hEithir's assertion that O'Flaherty wanted to live his life as a professional writer or the importance of Ó Conaire's impact on his philosophy and outlook (Conneely, 2011, 35–47).

Nevertheless, 2013 marks the 87th anniversary of the production on the Abbey stage, and a reexamination of *Dorchadas* seems long overdue. It is time to cast additional light on Liam O'Flaherty's Irish-language fiction and this singular moment in Irish-language theatre that brought together some of the most important and influential individuals and institutions associated with the Irish language in the Free State: Pádraic Ó Conaire, Liam O'Flaherty, León Ó Broin, Piaras Béaslaí, Daniel Corkery, An Gúm, An Comhar Drámaíochta. *Dorchadas* may have been an exception text, an aberration for its cultural environment, but its production history and the reverberations it sent through political, social, linguistic, and cultural networks were profound. Ó Siadhail notes *Dorchadas* was 'the most controversial play produced by An Comhar Drámaíochta', and it is arguably among, if not at the fore of, the most controversial Irish-language plays of the Free State era. In studying it, what it represented, proposed and opposed, we illuminate the Free State's social relations and power structures.

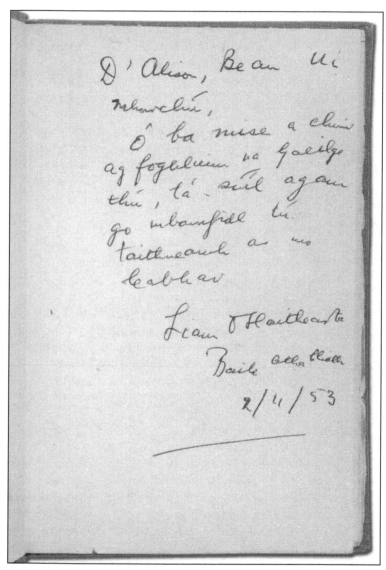

D'Ailíse, Bean Uí
Mhurchú,

Ó ba mise a chuir
ag foghluim na Gaeilge
thú, tá súil agam
go mbainfidh tú
taitneamh as mo
leabhar

Liam Ó Flaithearta
Baile Átha Cliath
2/4/53

Courtesy of Between the Covers Rare Books, Inc

1   Michael appears to have been born around 1846 and Margaret around 1855. They married in 1873; the 1911 census recorded that they were married 39 years and that 14 children had been born while only 11 remained alive. The three eldest girls (reportedly Mary, Margaret and Catherine) had emigrated to the United States by 1896. The younger girls were educated in various mainland convents as part of a Gaelic League project: Julia (Wicklow), Lil (Dundalk), Delia (Dundalk). Lil and Delia qualified from St. Mary's Training College, Belfast, and taught in that city. Annie retuned to teach on Aran, much to the consternation of the local clergy who sought to prevent, if not curtail, her brother's visits. (Mac an Iomaire 2001, 32–33). In 1911 Agnes registered her surname as 'O'Flaherty' rather than 'Flaherty'. For the family's comparative prosperity, see Peter Costello, *Liam O'Flaherty's Ireland* (1996), 13. See also Ó hEithir (1977, 65–76).

2   'Occupation, it turns out, is inaccurate as the revolutionaries were asked to leave the premises after having obtained its use deceitfully for one day from the manager, a Mr Kaye. Even at this early stage of his public career O'Flaherty had a strong sense of drama; he invited the police to intervene and "carry us out in their arms to their *Black Marias* if they liked"'. See Allen 2009, 15.

3   Other committee members included Seán Mac an tSaoir, J. Carroll, E. Mallon, and Pádraic Ó Flaithbheartaigh/Ó Fatharta. See Ó hEithir 1977, 73–74.

4   For the Battle of Dublin, see Peter Cottrell, *The Irish Civil War 1922–23* (2008), 35–59.

5   In a letter to Garnett (November 1923) O'Flaherty referred to a Dr Hallissey, a former schoolmate who was now a doctor in London. Hallissey had offered to intercede with friends in the Free State government to have O'Flaherty's works translated into Irish for use in the Department of Education (Kelly 1996, 56). Might this proposition have sparked O'Flaherty's subsequent return to writing in Irish? For O'Flaherty's decision to write, and later to cease to write, in Irish, see Risteárd Ó Glaisne, 'Rogha Teanga: Ó Flaithearta agus an Ghaeilge', *Comhar*, 39.6: 16–17; Tomás de Bhaldraithe, 'Liam Ó Flaitheartha: Aistritheoir', *Comhar*,

May 1967; Tomás de Bhaldraithe, 'Liam O'Flaherty: Translator', *Éire-Ireland*, 3.2; Nollaig Mac Congáil, 'Nóta faoi shaothar Gaeilge Liam Uí Fhlaithearta', *Comhar*, 40.6:17. See also Brian Ó Conchubhair, 'Liam Ó Flaithearta agus Scríobh na Gaeilge: Ceist Airgid nó Cinneadh Chonradh na Gaeilge?', *New Hibernia Review/Iris Éireannach Nua*, 4.2: 116–40.

6   O'Flaherty spent some time in 1928 with Mary Garman and Roy Campbell at their farmhouse in Tour de Vallier, near Martinque, France.

7   The cast included: Lars Hanson, Lya de Putti, Warwick Ward, Carl Harbord, Dennis Wyndham, Janice Adair, Daisy Campbell, Craighall Sherry, Ellen Pollock, and Johnny Butt. The film was also released in the United Kingdom in a silent version directed by Arthur Robison and starring Lya De Putti, Lars Hanson, Warwick Ward and Carl Harbord in 1929. Jules Dassin based his 1968 movie *Up Tight!* on O'Flaherty's *The Informer*, transposing the drama to a Black Panther Cleveland where Martin Luther King, Jr.'s assassination in April 1968 replaces the Irish War of Independence.

8   RKO purchased the rights for $2,500 but resisted Ford's efforts to produce it as early as 1930. Ford finally persuaded RKO, who agreed to a tight schedule of less than 20 days and a budget of $243,000. The film did not prove an instant hit, but rapturous reviews created a financial success and established Ford's critical reputation. In addition to Oscars for McLaglen, Ford, and Max Steiner, Dudley Nichols received the Oscar for Best Screenplay but refused it in solidarity with his fellow writers who had left the Academy of Motion Picture Arts and Sciences over union disputes. Patrick Byrne writes that when *The Informer* premiered in Paris, London, and New York, O'Flaherty was tucked away in Davy Byrne's on Duke Street, much to the consternation of reporters who sought an interview (Byrne n.d., 58).

9   For Ó hAnluain's role as editor of *Comhar* in enticing O'Flaherty back to writing in Irish, see Costello 1996, 105, and Ó hAnluain, 'A writer who bolstered the Irish revival', *The Irish Times*, 8 September 1984, 7.

10 See Pat Sheeran, 'Beastly Loot', *Comhar*, 43.12: 40–42. See also Costello 1996, 113–14. 'At this time he was also visited from time to time by Fr. Dermod McCarthy of the pro-Cathedral, who thought he had reconciled Liam with the Catholic Church. But in all honesty Liam was well beyond giving any informed consent to such a profession'.

11 Costello suggests the destruction and loss of correspondence from this period has distorted Garnett's importance. See Costello 1996, 47.

12 *The Irish Times* reports that Edmund Curtis attended a celebration of An Comhar Drámaíochta's third season (1926) on Saturday 24 April. 'At Roberts' Café, Grafton Street, Dublin, last Saturday evening, the Gaelic Players held a reception to commemorate the successful close of their third season at the Abbey Theatre. Among the large assembly of guests were the Speaker of the Dáil and Mrs. Hayes, Mr. and Mrs. R. Mulcahy, the Accountant-General and Mrs. Fitzgerald and Professor Edmund Curtis, M.A., T.C.D. The following contributed musical items: Máire Ní Oisín, Gráinne Nic Cathasaigh, T.J. Flynn, S. Flynn, M. Sugrue, and Seam (sic) O'Beirn'. (*The Irish Times*, 1 May, 1926, 12) Peter Kavanagh describes Roberts' Café in the 1940s as follows: 'Every Saturday morning Grafton Street was the place to be … At the top near the Green was Roberts, moderately fashionable. In the middle was Bewleys, a student hang-out, and near the bottom was Mitchells which was highly fashionable. Mitchells has much ironwork in the entrance, much glass and very high ceilings with chandeliers. In those days only the richest and most chic people dared enter. It was not any more expensive than the others but it had an aura about it, which kept the lower class out. Just below Mitchells was Jammets French restaurant. Very expensive. More of a night place than the coffee houses we speak of. Big commercial deals might be settled there but the coffee houses were for romances' (Kavanagh 2000, 115).

13 For Ó Conaire, see Ní Chionnaith 1995, Ó Cathasaigh 2007, and Riggs 1994.

14 Pádraic Ó Conaire perished in Dublin on 6 October 1928, two days after taking leave of O'Flaherty's cottage. See A.

Ní Chnáimhín, *Pádraic Ó Conaire* (Baile Átha Cliath, Oifig an tSoláthair 1947, 104–5).

15 Pádraic Ó Conaire (1882–1928), an accomplished author in Irish, best known for his collections of short stories and 1910 novel *Deoraíocht*. For Ó Conaire as a dramatist, see Pádraig Ó Siadhail, *Bairbre Rua agus Drámaí Eile* (Indreabhán, Cló Iar-Chonnachta, 1989). W.P. Ryan referenced the work of Ó Conaire in a review of Maurice Bourgeois' book *Synge and the Irish Theatre* ('the grim and what might be called Ibsenian Connacht interpreted in the writings of Padraic O Conaire') in *The Bookman*, December 1913, 170. See also W.P. Ryan, 'Drama and Democracy', *The Bookman*, August 1929, 271. In *The Athenaeum* (13 August 1920), W.B.W. wrote 'Only one Irish writer, I believe – Mr. Padraic O'Conaire – enjoys anything like a European reputation'.

16 For touring drama groups, see O'Leary 2004, 477–84. This notion is a clear echo of Ó Conaire's earlier project. See Pádraic Ó Conaire, 'Drámaí', *The Irishman*, 28 September 1918, in Gearóid Denvir (ed.) *Aistí Phádraic Uí Chonaire* (Gaillimh, Cló Chois Fharraige 1978, 128–30).

17 Gearóid Ó Lochlainn (1884–1970) was born in Liverpool, England. He spoke several languages, including Irish, which he learned from a native speaker when his family returned to Ireland. Active in amateur acting in Dublin prior to enrolling in university at Copenhagen in 1904, he later worked in the Danish silent film industry. In addition to being a founding member of An Comhar Drámaíochta, he was also a founding member of the Gate Theatre and a director for many years. Mícheál Mac Liammóir numbered him among the three people functioning within Irish who understood drama, the others being Mac Liammóir and Pól Ó Fearghail. See Gearóid Ó Lochlainn, *Ealaín na hAmharclainne* (Clódhanna Teo., 1966). See also Breathnach and Ní Mhurchú 1992, 115–7. Sisson describes how Madame Bannard Cogley, 'founder and hostess of a weekly cabaret club in Harcourt Street, and the actor Gearóid Ó Lochlainn had been talking about establishing a theatre company when they were introduced by A.J. Leventhal to Mac Liammóir and Edwards in early 1928. Mac Liammóir and Edwards had been appointed directors

of the Taibhdhearc Theatre in Galway but were looking for a theatre in Dublin' (Sisson 2010, 146–7).

18   *The Times* (London) reported (20 July 1925, 5) that among the undefended divorce cases heard in Court 1 by J. Hill were Curtis v. Curtis and O'Flaherty. K.A. Nealon Walsh wrote to the *Irish Independent* on July 22, 1925 (8), 'to say the St. Valerie near Bray in the Curtis Divorce suit in London is not St. Valerie's Convalescent Home, Dargle Road, Bray'. It is unclear if this case is related to the Curtis v. Curtis and O'Flaherty case, but it would nevertheless have drawn further attention.

19   Shelia Lahr recalls in her memoir *Yealm*: 'My mother had been a member of the British Socialist Party, which following the Russian Revolution, dissolved itself into the newly formed Communist Party of Great Britain. My father had always considered himself an Anarchist, anarchism originally having been part of the Communist movement. However, both of my parents were distressed at the shooting down of the rebellious sailors at Kronstadt and although they remained at that time within the Communist Party, they became more and more uneasy as Stalinism took hold. This unease bringing in its train cynicism was to lead to my father's expulsion from the Party'.
http://www.militantesthetix.co.uk/yealm/yealm2.htm (accessed 19 September 2011).

20   K.S. Bhat was an Indian doctor (possibly with a practice in London) and a customer at the Progressive Bookshop who befriended the Lahrs (private correspondence with Sheila Leslie). Bhat combined an interest in labour politics and fiction. Among his titles are *Labour in India: Being an Address to the Irish Labour Party and Trade Union Congress delivered at Drogheda, 5 August 1919* (Irish Labour Party and Trade Union Congress 1919); *Panini* (E. Archer 1926); *When we were very green: with apologies to Mr. A.A. Milne* (E. Archer 1929); *Soma: June 1931* (K. S. Bhat/E. Lahr 1931); and *An Indictment of Slave Labour* (Workers Welfare of India c. 1930).

21   The magazine folded in 1927. Lahr's financial position continued to deteriorate. Convicted of receiving stolen

books in 1935, he served six months in prison. A bombing raid in May 1941 destroyed the premises.

22 Garnett's intervention secured a Royal Literary Fund (£200) for O'Flaherty at this stage.

23 James Sullivan Starkey (1879–1958). *The Dublin Magazine* was published by New Square Publications and ran from August 1923–August 1925 and again from 1926–1958.

24 On 15 July 2008, Christie's auctioneers sold Roberts' original sketch for £1,188. Lahr published additional texts by O'Flaherty in the following years: *Joseph Conrad: An Appreciation* (London, E. Lahr 1930, Blue Moon Booklets No. 1) – 100 signed copies; *The Child of God* (London, E. Archer 1926) – 125 signed copies, 25 copies with William Roberts' portrait of the author; *A Cure for Unemployment* (London, E. Lahr 1931, Blue Moon Booklets No. 8). See Paul A. Doyle, *Liam O'Flaherty: An Annotated Bibliography* (New York, The Whitson Publishing Company 1972, 3–4).

25 In April 1926, William and Sarah Roberts lived at an address that is variously given as 59 College Road and 59 Haverstock Hill (private correspondence with Robert Davenport).

26 In Shelia Lahr's memoir *Yealm*, she refers to 'my mother's friend Dornan ... for the short time we live in Fairbridge Road our family becomes extended by my father's sister Tante Maria and Margot, the illegitimate daughter of my mother's friend Dornan. Margot, a child some five years older than me'. See http://www.militantesthetix.co.uk/yealm/CONTENTS.htm (accessed 17 September 2011).

27 Max Kramer (?–1916), an artist who trained under Repin in St. Petersburg, and his wife, Celia, an opera singer and expert on folk songs, fled the Russian Pogram from Klincy, a small town in the Ukraine, in 1900. They settled in the Jewish community anchored by the textile and clothing firms in Leeds. Max worked in photographic portraiture and struggled to provide for his family as his eyesight deteriorated. The family had five children: Jacob, Leah, Millie, Isaac, and Sarah. Sarah was the first to be born in England (29 July 1900). Jacob attended Darley Street Council School and night art classes at Leeds School of Art. In 1912 the Jewish Educational Aid Society secured a loan

allowing him to attend London's Slade School of Fine Art, then enjoying the apogee of its history, where he befriended C.R.W. Nevinson, Augustus John, David Bomberg, Mark Gertler, and William Roberts (b. 5 June 1895) as well as members of what would become the Ben Uri Society of Art. Sarah modelled for Jacob and William, who had left school at the age of 14 to become apprenticed to a poster-designing and advertising firm before winning a scholarship to the Slade in 1910. After Sarah finished her service in the army, she and William married. He died at the Royal Free Hospital in London on January 20, 1980.

28 Born Vivian Rees Davies at Tonypandy in a coal-mining area of Glamorgan, Rhys Davies (1901–1978) initially left the Rhondda valley for Cardiff but settled in London, where he spent most of his life publishing in English while setting his novels and short stories in Wales. Lahr published his early work in the second issue of *The New Coterie* (Spring 1926) with a frontispiece portrait by Roberts. Roberts also drew the cover for *The Withered Root*, Davies' first novel. E. Archer published his *The Song of Songs and Other Stories* in 1927, and O'Flaherty penned a laudatory introduction to *The Stars, The World, and The Women* (London, William Jackson 1930). Davies obligingly returned the compliment with an introduction to O'Flaherty's *The Wild Swan and Other Stories* (London, Joiner & Steele 1932). *Print of a Hare's Foot: An Autobiographical beginning by Rees Davies* (1969), Davies' autobiography, describes a 1927 visit to Lahr's birthplace in the company of Roberts, H.E. Bates, and Lahr.

29 Roberts' 1920 composition 'Taking the Oath' seems undeniably Irish in content and raises an interesting, if tangential, link with O'Flaherty, who would author a memoir of Tim Healy, the Irish politician first appointed as Governor-General of the Irish Free State in 1922. The Oath of Allegiance, by which one pledged loyalty to 'the Irish Free State Constitution and faithfulness to King George V, his heirs and successors in law in virtue of the common citizenship of Ireland with Great Britain and her adherence to and membership of the group of nations forming the British Commonwealth of nations', had to be sworn before

Healy or his representative. The controversial oath would prove a vital factor in instigating the Irish Civil War.

30 An Comhar Drámaíochta also offered a number of public lectures on drama. See Ó Súilleabháin 1972, 3.

31 O'Flaherty had used the occasion of the performance to pen an attack on Yeats in AE's *Irish Statesman* on 20 February 1926. See Allen 2009, 53.

32 First produced on 1 November 1900 in Belfast and subsequently on 27 August 1901 by Frank Fay, Willie Fay, and the Ormonde Dramatic Group in the Antient Concert Rooms, Dublin. Breathnach and Ó Murchú suggest it may be the first staged Irish-language play. See Breathnach and Ó Murchú 1986, 38.

33 Constance P. Anderson, *The Courting of the Widow Malone*. See Ní Mhurchú and Breathnach 2007, 147.

34 Born in Dublin and best known as editor of *Peig*, Máire Ní Chinnéide (1878–1967) composed a number of plays, including: *An Cochall Draoidheachta* (1938), *Cáit Ní Dhuibhir* (1938), and *Scéal an Tí* (1953). Cumann Camógaíochta na nGael/The Camogie Association of Ireland elected her as its first president in 1904–1905.

35 Máire Ní Oisín was a core member of An Comhar Drámaíochta. She acted in Mac Liammóir's production of Béaslaí's *An Bhean Chrodha* (Gate Theatre, 27 January 1931); Béaslaí's *Fear na Fógraidheachta* (Peacock, 16 October 1934); Mac Liammóir's production of Máire Ní Shíthe's translation of Moliere's *Le Bourgeois Gentilhomme* (Gate Theatre, 25 November 1930); León Ó Broin's *An Chlosgcíobhaí* (5 February 1929); and *Na Cluig* (5 December 1933). She appeared regularly on 2RN's 6:15pm program *Uair i dTír na nÓg* from 1928–1930. *The Irish Independent* (16 December 1939) lists her as a 'typist' with Rannóg an Aistriúcháin. Her photo appears with several members of An Comhar Drámaíochta in the *Irish Independent* (12 November 1923, 3). The *Irish Independent* (24 September 1928, 8) notes that 'she represented the Western tradition' at the Siamsa.

36 Another core member of An Comhar Drámaíochta's ensemble, Máire Ní Shíocháin/Shíothcháin translated T.C. Murray's *Birthright* as *Oidhreacht* and played the part of

Mary when it was produced in March 1916 at the Irish Theatre, Hardwicke St.

37   Muiris Ó Cathain (1890–1960) was a Kerry man who taught in Dublin and fought in the War of Independence. He began acting in 1914 and was a pivotal figure in the foundation of An Comhar Drámaíochta.

38   Born in Wexford, William Richard English Murphy (W.R.E. Murphy, 1890–1975) enlisted in 1915 as an officer in the British Army but supported the IRA during the War of Independence. He was appointed Deputy Leader in the Free State Army during the Civil War. At the Civil War's conclusion, he was placed in charge of the Dublin Metropolitan Police and subsequently became Deputy Leader of An Garda Síochána. He retired from the force in 1955. He was instrumental in securing Frank Duff's campaign to close the Monto district in Dublin during Lent on 12 March 1925. In England, nightclubs that had mushroomed in the aftermath of the 1921 Licensing Acts were vigorously policed and regularly raided. See Taylor, 2007, 49.

39   See Greta Jones and Elizabeth Malcolm, *Medicine, Disease and the State in Ireland, 1650–1940* (Cork University Press 1999, 262–3). Monto is the setting for O'Flaherty's short story 'Unclean'.

40   See Brian Ó Conchubhair, 'Liam Ó Flaithearta agus Scríobh na Gaeilge: Ceist Airgid nó Cinneadh Chonradh na Gaeilge?', *New Hibernia Review/Iris Éireannach Nua*, 4.2: 116–40. See also John Cronin, 'Liam O'Flaherty and *Dúil*', *New Hibernia Review/Iris Éireannach Nua*, 7.1: 45–55.

41   Fiachra Éilgeach's (Ristéard Ó Foghludha) translation of *The Courting of the Widow Malone* (1922). An Comhar Drámaíochta produced this one-act comedy on 16 February 1925, according to Playography na Gaeilge. Cast members included Máire Ní Oisín, Máire Ní Shíothcháin, Gearóid Ó Lochlainn, and Tadhg Ó Scanaill. The text was published in 1927.

42   'The second play was Mrs. Constance Powell-Anderson's ever delightful little comedy *Wooing the Widow*; and here Máire Ní Oisín, as a roguish girl, who helps the lovers to woo in poetry, was at her best. Mr. O'Scanail was welcome in his old part of the fierce wooer. The piece is among the

best in the players' repertoire' (*The Irish Times*, 2 March 1926, 5).

43   Ní Shíothcháin/Shíocháin translated T.C. Murray's *Birthright* as *Oidhreacht*.

44   'Noel' was León Ó Broin's *non de plume*. It may be that 'Neol' was an error by the typesetter in place of 'Noel' and that Ó Broin penned this review.

45   For the plays published by An Comhar Drámaíochta at this time, see Pádraig Ó Siadhail, *Stair Dhrámaíocht na Gaeilge 1900–1970* (Indreabhán, Cló Iar-Chonnachta 1993, 64–65). Among the plays published by An Gúm were Piaras Béaslaí's *An Sgaothaire agus Cúig Drámaí Eile* (1929), Fiachra Éilgeach's *Naoi nGearra Chluiche* (1930), León Ó Broin's *An Mhallacht agus Trí Drámaí* (1931), Lady Gregory's *Dubhairt Sé Dabhairt Sé* (1931, translated by An Seabhac), J.M. Synge's *Deirdre an Bhróin* (1933, translated by León Ó Broin), and Douglas Hyde's *Casadh an tSúgáin* (1934) and *Maistín an Bhéarla* (1934). The paucity of published plays in Irish is evident in Risteárd de hAe's, *Clár Litridheacht na Nua-Ghaeilge 1850–1936*, which lists 106 published plays – original and translated – in Irish.

46   See Brian Ó Conchubhair, 'Liam Ó Flaithearta agus Scríobh na Gaeilge: Ceist Airgid nó Cinneadh Chonradh na Gaeilge?', *New Hibernia Review/Iris Éireannach Nua* 4:2: 116–140.

47   Frank O'Connor would later reside in the same apartment block as O'Flaherty at Wilton Court, 'but while his apartment was alive with comings and goings, O'Flaherty gained the reputation of a solitary' (Costello 1996, 97).

48   See Edgar M. Slotkin, 'Two Irish literary manuscripts in the Mid-West', *Éigse* 25 (1991), 56–80. My thanks to Dr. Meidhbhín Ní Úrdail for bringing this article to my attention.

49   In 2010 the rare book firm Peter Harrington (100 Fulham Road, Chelsea, London, SW3 6HS) offered for sale: 'First edition, first impression. One of 10 unbound copies printed simultaneously with the limited edition of 100 copies. This copy inscribed by the author on the outer leaf "Liam O'Flaherty. This is one of 12 copies" Stock code: 60892. Price: £750'.

DARKNESS

A Tragedy in Three Acts

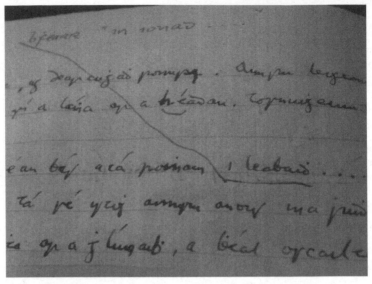

Sample of O'Flaherty's editing from Kentucky manuscript

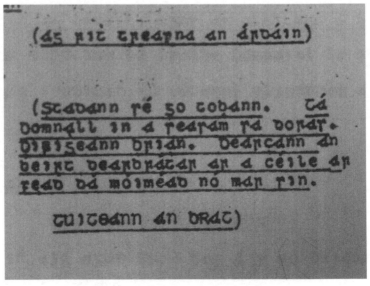

Final page of Galway manuscript

Final page of Act 1 (Kentucky manuscript)

CAST

MARY: an old woman
DARK DANIEL: Mary's eldest surviving son
MERRY BRIAN: Mary's young surviving son
BEAUTIFUL BRIDGET: Margaret's daughter
PROUD MARGARET: Bridget's mother

ACT I

SCENE:

*A thatched three-roomed cabin with whitewashed walls
cover the rear of the stage, with an opening on either side of
it. A dark painted door is in the centre of the wall, with a
window on either side of the door, at equal distances from
the door and the gables. The roof of the house retreats at a
sharp slope out of sight. In the yard in front of the house
there are large granite rocks scattered here and there. A
rough track crosses the front of the yard. Rough tools, used
by primitive peasants to root up the earth are thrown by the
wall of the house.*

*It is midday and there is a dead calm, with a dull
brooding feeling in the darkened air. As the curtain rises*
MARY, *an old woman, is sitting on a rock to the right of the
door. She is knitting. Her son,* DARK DANIEL, *comes out of
the house. He stands near her, his arms folded, gazing ahead
gloomily. The old woman drops her knitting in her lap and
looks at him for a moment. Then she speaks.*

MARY: Where are you going, Daniel?

DANIEL: I have to change the cow from the Fairy Field.
    She has nothing there to eat and the well among the
    flags is dry. I will put her in the Great Crag. She'll
    have grass there to drag from the deep fissures
    while the drought lasts. And there is water for her
    in the rock pools.

MARY: You should have done that since morning.

She takes up her knitting and bends over it.

DANIEL: (*Shaking his hands above his head and turning to
    the left*). Ach!

MARY: (*In a nagging voice*). It is midday now and you
    haven't stirred from the hearthstone since the
    milking of the cow.

DANIEL: (*Looking behind him at her*). Go to the devil.

MARY: May your prayer not be answered! Isn't the narrow field to be weeded and the weeds as tall as sticks there for a fortnight?

DANIEL: (*Turning towards her savagely*). Let it be. I don't care any more for the sowing of Spring or for the reaping of the Autumn. Let it rot. Let the weeds smother it. May it not grow by day nor swell with the dew of night. What is it to me?

MARY: (*Throwing back her body and stretching forth her hands, aghast*). Son of perdition! Son of madness!

DANIEL: (*Crouching over her, with his right hand raised arrogantly aloft*). Shut up! Listen to my talk. It's not with madness I am speaking but with the darkness that is fallen on my heart. Am I not now for twenty years harrowing the earth since my father and my three brothers were drowned and I a lad. Harrowing and rooting for you and for Brian, the pet of your old age?

MARY: (*Rising and menacing him with her two hands*). Ungainly lout! Brian is the cause of your madness. You hate my beautiful son that was formed in the same womb as you. You are jealous of the beauty of his body.

DANIEL: (*Suddenly striking his forehead and making for a rock, crouching*). Mother, there is darkness on my heart and I don't know what I say. (*He sits on the rock*). I'm an ungainly lout and there is darkness on my heart.

MARY *comes to him. She puts a hand on his head.*

MARY: (*Softly*). Son! Forgive my word. I spoke in anger. Even if he is an ungainly lout, a son is beautiful to his mother. Am I not proud of the strength of your hand and the eagerness of your eye, when you are tearing up the grassy earth in Spring, putting black soil on the seed. But you are sick, my treasure. Tell me the cause of your sorrow. Speak my share of the world.

DANIEL: (*Downcast*). I have no sickness but a sickness that cannot be cured.

MARY: Speak, son. There is a healing herb in every mother's heart. There is no profit in hiding sorrow. Let it from you softly with the words of your mouth.

DANIEL: (*Rising suddenly and going from her*). Let me alone. I cannot make my complaint to you. (*He stands. He looks at the sky. He raises his voice*). I will make my lamentation to the birds of the air and to the beasts of the mountains and to the insects that are murmuring in the grass of the earth. I have no kinship with people. I'm an ungainly lout.

MARY: (*In terror*). What queer talk is this?

She sits, awed, on the rock from which DANIEL *rose.*

DANIEL: (*Returning to his mother*). Whoever spoke to me with love? Whoever smiled at me walking the road or gathering seaweed on the shore? Whoever made conversation with me on a grassy mound when the red sun was drowning in the sea?

He stumbles up and down the yard, raving as he speaks.

MARY: (*Almost in tears as she rocks herself*). O, Son! Son! What ails you? What ails you at all? Isn't it well I know the hardship and the misery you have got from your life?

DANIEL: (*Halting suddenly and crying savagely*). A hag's devilry!

MARY: Going with the dawn in winter when the hoar frost was like a cloak of poison on the crag and the white sea torn with the wind.

DANIEL: (*Roving up and down again*). Yes! You can talk now, but the day of storm is not the day to make a house secure. Now the devil's game is played and I am wounded. It's your fault.

MARY: My fault, son!

DANIEL: (*Standing before her*). Yes. It's your fault with the way you petted Brian. Was I not standing lonely on the desolate shore, gathering seaweed for the sowing of Spring, up to my neck in the freezing sea, with a pitchfork in my hand, stooping for the red strands of seaweed that would be carried past me on the tide, while he was lying cuddled in the blankets?

MARY: Don't blame me for that. Blame yourself as well. Didn't you, too, shelter him from hardship? Don't I remember the night well when you shed tears over his bed and he a boy; when the red light of sickness was on his cheeks and a poisonous cough smothering him?

DANIEL: Well? And what sickness has he now? Going lightheaded among the women and making a rake of himself all over the island without doing a stroke of work?

MARY: Doesn't he fish?

DANIEL: What good is fishing?

MARY: (*Looking up the track suddenly*). Whist! Here comes Beautiful Bridget and her daughter, Proud Margaret.

BEAUTIFUL BRIDGET *and* PROUD MARGARET *enter from the left.*

MARY: God be with ye. How are you, Bridget?

BRIDGET: God and Mary with ye. Oh! Indeed I am not very well. There are signs of thunder in the eastern sky and the sea is growling loudly in the Fountain

Hole. That is a sign of a storm. There will be a thunderstorm to-night.

BRIDGET *sits on a rock near* MARY. *She peers closely at* DANIEL. MARGARET *stands a little behind the women, near* DANIEL, *looking at him coquettishly.* DANIEL *does not look at her. He scowls and goes to the doorpost against which he leans.*

MARY: (*Beginning to knit again*). I fear the thunder since Coleman and my three sons were drowned.

BRIDGET: God have mercy on their souls! It was about this time they were drowned. I mind it well.

MARY: They are drowned now twenty years.

DANIEL: They are, and I am twenty years in hardship.

MARY: (*Rocking*). The day was so calm when they went westwards beneath the towering cliffs that the prow of their coracle did not break a basin full of froth on the oily surface of the sea.

BRIDGET: (*Also rocking with polite affected woe*). The dome of heaven was spotless.

DANIEL: It's easy for ye to sorrow.

MARY: Then a whirlwind gathered in the east.

BRIDGET: It came westwards over the Hill of Slaughter in a black mass, with its sound rocking the sky.

MARY: It lashed the sea. There was nothing to be seen but the white froth rising through the darkness; white ghosts of perdition rising from the blackness of the sea.

DANIEL: Foo!

He paces with cumbersome haste to a rock and plants his left foot on it and rests his chin in his palm. There is a slight pause. The women rock.

BRIDGET: They were never found.

MARY: Never. The brightness of my life was never found, neither he nor my three sons. Their graves are buried in the deep. And my heart is buried with them. Oh! My sorrow!

DANIEL: Death is not a cause for sorrow, but a cause for joy. I, I am in hardship.

BRIDGET: Say not so Daniel. The sun does not shine in the darkness of death.

MARY: (*Raising her head and wiping her eyes*). Do you hear him Bridget? Isn't this a curse that is following me? My man and my three sons drowned on me and the two darling ones that are left to me growing anger in their hearts against each other.

BRIDGET: (*To Daniel*). What's this I hear?

DANIEL: Hag's talk. It's not anger that's growing in my heart. Nothing is growing in my heart, but everything is rotting in it from day to day.

MARY: A curse! A curse!

BRIDGET: (*In pretend anger*). That's not a proper answer to the sorrowful moan of a sick heart.

DANIEL: It's not a curse, but the way you petted Brian. Small credit to him to have a fine body. (*He turns fiercely to* MARGARET). His body is a body that never worked. (*He stretches forth his hands*). But I am crooked with hardship.

BRIDGET: (*Rising*). Whist darling. I think there is a cure for your sorrow. Leave it to me and to your mother. Come into the house, Mary. I have a whisper for you about that thing the other day. Margaret speak to Daniel out here, my treasure. Come on, Mary. There is nothing as healing as the soft whisper of a maiden when there is a wound in a young man's heart. Come in. Let us go in.

MARY: (*Entering the door*). In the name of God!

The two women disappear into the house. The door is closed. DANIEL *looks after them curiously.* MARGARET *watches* DANIEL, *her eyes smiling.*

DANIEL: What work is this they have on foot?

MARGARET: (*Advancing towards him swaying at the hips*). How do I know? What made you so cross, Daniel?

DANIEL: (*Regarding her fiercely, with his legs spread*). She devil!

He turns and walks from her two steps. He stands. Then he sits suddenly on a rock and puts his head between his hands. MARGARET *follows him slowly, seductively. She stands beside him.*

MARGARET: You are a foolish man, Daniel. (*Pause*). Look at me. (*He looks at her gloomily*). Don't you like me?

DANIEL: Proud Margaret! Your face is beautiful, but there is no pity in your heart. Your heart is hard like this rock.

He strikes the rock on which he sits.

MARGARET: (*Laughing with her throat bent backwards*). O! How sweet your tongue is!

DANIEL: What good is to me to look at you? It's not at me your mouth ever smiled. Mocking and temptation. Temptress!

MARGARET: (*Drawing closer*). How clumsy your speech is! (*Softly*). I often smiled at you, Daniel, but –

DANIEL: Mocker!

MARGARET: But your head was stooping, as if it were tethered to the earth. Do you hear?

He rises and he is moving away from her when she touches him gently. He starts violently and becomes rigid.

MARGARET: Don't go. Wait. Listen. I'll tell you something.

DANIEL: What?

MARGARET: You're wasting your life, with your head to the earth from morning till night. Your life is lonely without a woman. That's the darkness that has fallen on you. (*He begins to tremble, looking at the ground. She takes up his right hand in both hers*). Look at the strength of your hand. Is there anything in the world as wonderful as the great strength of a man's hand? Look at the big fingers that would smother the breath in a lion's throat. Look at the fair hairs growing as thickly as on a woman's head. (*She steps a little away from him. He takes a step after her*). I saw you one day seizing a bullock that went mad with the heat. You put a hand on his horn and another in his nostrils. You twisted his head. I was standing behind the wall among the shrieking women. I heard the snapping of the muscles like the snapping of a moored boat's cables in a storm. And the mad bullock was trembling and you were crouching over him … just as you are trembling before me now, Daniel.

DANIEL: Margaret. Say one word to me. Do.

MARGARET: What word?

DANIEL: Speak from your heart.

MARGARET: How?

DANIEL: Are you promised to Brian?

MARGARET: (*Laughingly*). I promised to Brian!

DANIEL: Yes. Speak.

MARGARET: What put that in your head?

DANIEL: Are they not in there making the match?

MARGARET: For whom?

DANIEL: You and Brian.

MARGARET: Are you out of your mind?

DANIEL: Are you promised to him, I say?

MARGARET: What is it to you?

He seizes her hand. She gasps, terrified. She snatches away her hand. He tries to seize her. She beats him with her hands and cries.

MARGARET: Don't put your beast's paws on me.

She rushes from him. He stands, dumbfounded by the insult and his passion, his hands outstretched, looking at his hands.

DANIEL: A beast's paws is it? (*Fiercely*). I'd tear –

Just then the voice of MERRY BRIAN *is heard approaching, singing as he comes.*

BRIAN: (*At a distance and gradually approaching, is heard singing a merry song, a folk-song. Then he enters, halts and stops singing*). Proud Margaret here! The sun is jealous.

MARGARET: (*Laughing*). It's not Merry Brian you should be called, but Brian of the sweet tongue. Where were you?

BRIAN: I was fishing off the reef of the yellow cliff.

MARGARET: Where is the fish?

BRIAN: I left them on the flag to be cleaned.

MARGARET: Did you catch much?

BRIAN: Very little. There is some evil in the air.

MARGARET: A bad fisherman always blames the weather.

BRIAN: It may be so. But still there is something queer going to happen. When we put to sea at dawn, the sea was like a smooth floor, as if oil were spilt on it. And now the rock-birds are hiding in their holes. The seagulls are tacking through the sky and they are screaming. The fish have fled out into the deep. There is nothing to be found but dog-fish, the refuse of the sea.

MARGARET: It's small wonder for the fish to run from you.

BRIAN: Why?

MARGARET: If you were singing like a choking cock.

BRIAN: (*Pursuing her*). Ha! You little devil! Wait till I –

DANIEL *suddenly steps in front of* BRIAN. BRIAN *halts. They stare at one another.*

DANIEL: Let her alone. You can't fool about in my yard with the women of the village, you scoundrel.

BRIAN: Your yard is it?

DANIEL: Yes, my yard.

BRIAN: It's not yours yet. It's mother's yard.

DANIEL: She wouldn't have house nor yard only for me, that's working for her and for you from morning till night, while you are raking around without profit.

BRIAN: Without profit? Isn't that the worse for myself, and not for you? Haven't you the land? Work it. I'm not putting in on you. The fishing is mine.

DANIEL: The land is mine is it? Don't I share the crops with you and the cow's milk and the sheep's wool?

BRIAN: Don't I share the fish with you?

DANIEL: You have fine talk, you ... you ... you ... but I'm wounded with hardship and it's you have the benefit.

BRIAN: Come now, brother, don't be telling your story to the women of the village.

MARGARET: Oh! I'm going.

BRIAN: Don't go, Margaret. Wait ...

He smiles at her.

DANIEL: You don't care what I say, but I'll make you care.

MARGARET: Oh! I'm going. It's I am vexing him.

BRIAN: Don't mind the lout.

DANIEL: A lout is it? By the horned devil …

He rushes at BRIAN. *They attack one another.* MARGARET *screams, calling for her mother. The old women rush out at the door. They seize the still struggling men.*

MARY: Daniel! Daniel! Don't strike. Don't strike.

DANIEL: (*In a yell*). Stand back.

BRIDGET: Separate them.

MARY: Catch his hands.

BRIAN: Let go my hands.

BRIDGET: Hold fast now.

They separate the men.

DANIEL: (*Held by the two women*). Let me to him. Ah-h.

They drag DANIEL *towards the house screaming. They enter the house. The door bangs shut.*

BRIAN: Foo! By the Stag of Hell! (*He laughs airily*). Were you afraid, Margaret?

MARGARET: (*Fearfully*). Every time I look at his two terrible hands I become afraid. He would only have to squeeze a person's throat with those hands and – (*she makes a gesture like being throttled*). But you pay heed to nothing.

BRIAN: What's the use of worrying about life? There is enough darkness in the night without darkening the day with care. While the sun shines my heart is happy.

MARGARET: Your heart! You have no heart.

BRIAN: Why?

MARGARET: You're a butterfly flitting from flower to flower.

BRIAN: No, but from girl to girl. That's what is worrying you maybe.

MARGARET: Oh! The conceit of him! Flit away. There isn't the strength of a man in your hand.

BRIAN: That may be. But a butterfly doesn't need strength to taste the sap of a flower; the sweet sap of woman.

MARGARET: You senseless mocker.

BRIAN: I'm not mocking but in earnest.

MARGARET: That may be, as you said yourself. They say you are only half a man.

BRIAN: (*Angrily*). Who said so?

MARGARET: Look at your little hands.

BRIAN *stretches forth his hands and looks at them.*

MARGARET: Your hands are like the little soft white hands of a woman.

She laughs. She flits to the left of the stage laughing and looking backwards at him. He rushes after her suddenly. He halts at the edge of the stage. He puts his hands in his hair. His face darkens with anger. Then his hands drop to his sides. His eyes and his mouth soften. The far-reaching light of love comes into his eyes. He begins to tremble slightly. He speaks softly, in a low voice.

BRIAN: What's coming over me? (*Pause*). My heart is beating loudly and a ... (*Pause*). Proud Margaret. (*Pause*). (*Then joyously*). Little Margaret ... My little treasure.

There is a short pause while he gazes in ecstasy. Then he starts as the door is opened. The two hags appear. They walk to the right of the stage conversing. They do not see BRIAN.

BRIDGET: That is the best thing for us to do.

MARY: There is no other woman I would rather have.

BRIDGET: And he is worthy of any woman, to sow and to reap and to protect a household.

MARY: Daniel is a good man, truly.

BRIDGET: And Margaret is as eager in a house as …

MARY: Oh! Indeed, you needn't tell me.

They disappear to the right.

BRIAN: (*Rushing across the stage*). Now the devil is done.

He halts suddenly. He sees DANIEL *standing in the doorway. The two brothers stare at one another.*

CURTAIN FALLS

NB Only thirty seconds interval between first and second Acts. There should be perfect silence in the theatre (no music).

ACT II

SCENE:

Same. BRIAN *is sitting outside the house on a rock, with his head between his hands, singing sadly a love song called 'Maureen De Barra'.* MARY *comes out of the house to him. It is evening. A thunderstorm threatens. It is already quite dusk.*

MARY: Arise my son. What use is it to be sorrowful? Come into the house and eat something. Come. Oh! My son! My son! Obey your mother. Don't break the heart in me. Come.

BRIAN: Let me alone, mother. Let me be.

MARY: (*Walking desolately out over the centre of the stage*). Dear! Dear! Was the darkness raised from Daniel's heart to cast it down on Brian's? He is gone now merrily to the cow while my little Brian –

BRIAN: (*Jumping up*). Is it any wonder for him to be merry? And you after enticing my girl from me so as to satisfy him.

MARY: (*Turning to him*). Don't say that, my treasure. How did I know that you were in love with her? Or in love with any woman? I thought it was how he was jealous of you about the work. If I had only known that ... (*making a hopeless gesture*) but what could be done? Oh! Brian my heart is sore. (*She sits on a rock*). Is this evil I have done instead of good? Great God of Glory answer me. Two darling sons and a mother that loves them both alike. Hard, hard is my lot.

She weeps aloud.

BRIAN: Mother! Mother! (*He rushes to her. He puts a hand on her shoulder*). Don't cry, mother. My heart is wounded when you cry. Listen, mother. Listen. I will do anything in the world for you, but don't cry.

MARY: (*Wiping her eyes*). Don't blame me, son. The tears broke under my eyelids in spite of me.

BRIAN: (*Kneeling on one knee*). It's my fault, mother. I'm not used to suffering. You and Daniel always sheltered me from suffering since I was born. But a flood tide of sorrow is now making a great cold lake around my heart. It is manifest now to me that this sorrow comes sometimes to every man's heart. Strength does not grow in the mind until sorrow has pierced the heart.

MARY: Brightness of brightness, how sweet is the sound of your voice.

BRIAN: Mother, you are ...

Suddenly he stops. He sees DANIEL *enter the stage from the right.*

BRIAN: Brother! (BRIAN *rises.* MARY *rises.* DANIEL *stands. The three of them gaze for a time. Then* BRIAN *approaches his brother*). Are you still angry with me, Daniel?

DANIEL *looks at him angrily at first. Then he looks at his mother. His face softens. He is fighting in his heart with anger and love for* BRIAN.

MARY: Speak to him, Daniel. I beg you, my son. Come together now. Gladden my heart. Gladden the sad heart of your mother – my pulse. I have only the two of you in the world.

DANIEL *begins to tremble, wiping his hands on his clothes. Then he speaks suddenly. His voice is wild and almost broken.*

DANIEL: I'm not angry with you, Brian.

MARY: Praise be the Great God of Glory. My heart is merry now. I will leave my darlings now to make your peace before they come to make the match.

They should be on their way now. I will go up the road before them.

She leaves the stage. The two brothers stand some time looking ahead. Their hands are behind their backs. Their fingers are twitching. At last DANIEL *speaks.*

DANIEL: There is terrible heat.

BRIAN *starts. He does not look at* DANIEL.

BRIAN: There is. The sky is darkening.

Another pause just as before.

BRIAN: Was it changing the cow you were?

DANIEL: Yes. (*Pause*). It won't be safe to go fishing to-night.

BRIAN: No. There is a great movement in the sea beyond the point of the Black Precipice.

Another pause. BRIAN *then attempts to approach his brother, but just then* DANIEL *also moves, attempting to approach* BRIAN. *They both start looking at one another. They stand trembling. Then* DANIEL *advances a pace. His face is gentle with love for* BRIAN. *His mouth was opening to speak when a loud voice was heard afar. Both brothers start, become rigid, listening.*

MARY: (*From afar*). A hundred thousand welcomes to you.

DANIEL: (*Excitedly*). She is coming.

BRIAN: (*Excitedly*). Daniel.

DANIEL *does not notice. He is listening.*

BRIAN: (*Louder, almost fiercely*). Daniel, I say. Does she love you?

DANIEL *turns towards him slowly, soft, weak, simple.*

DANIEL: Little brother! Let me have her. Let me have her. Let her not come between me and you. My –

He stops, hearing the voice of BEAUTIFUL BRIDGET *as she approaches the stage.*

BRIDGET: (*Approaching*). The sun is dim and gloomy. There is a shadow over its face, the dark shadow of evil filling the sky. (*She enters the stage and sees the two brothers*). May God protect you both.

DANIEL and BRIAN: And ye, too!

BRIDGET, MARY *and* MARGARET *walk across the stage.*

MARY: Let ye come into the house.

BRIDGET: Not yet. When there is anger in the heart it should be cast out under the great sky, where the soul can feel the beauty of the world. Peace must be made first, Mary. A match without goodwill is no match.

MARY: Oh! Put that out of your head, Bridget. If my two sons were jealous of one another, it's not so now. They have made their peace, praised be God.

BRIDGET: Is that true, Daniel?

DANIEL: That's true.

BRIDGET: Is that true, Brian?

BRIAN: It is, but –

BRIDGET: But what?

MARY: Brian! Brian! I beg you.

BRIDGET: Let him alone, I say.

DANIEL: You scoundrel, what are you –

MARY: Don't start on him, Daniel.

BRIAN: Let me have my say.

BRIDGET: This is no peace, Mary.

DANIEL: Don't blame me for it.

BRIAN: Let me speak, I say. I only want a word.

BRIDGET: Say the word.

BRIAN: I'd like to ask Margaret a question.

DANIEL: You devil, didn't you promise me …

BRIDGET: Patience, man alive.

BRIAN: I asked you a question you didn't answer.

DANIEL: You're a liar.

BRIDGET: Don't mind him, Brian. Ask your question.

There is a slight pause.

BRIAN: Margaret, are you in love with Daniel?

MARGARET *starts. She comes to the front of the stage in the centre. Her two hands are clasping her bosom. She gazes ahead. All look at her. They suddenly turn towards her as if by common intuition something strange had been made manifest to their minds; something that had been drawing them on but which they could not grasp until now. There is a long pause.*

BRIDGET: Speak child. (*Slowly, softly*). Didn't you tell me that you were willing to marry him?

MARGARET *turns towards them suddenly.*

MARGARET: I did but … (*In a low voice*). I don't know.

MARY: (*Angrily*). What's this?

BRIDGET: (*Angrily*). Daughter.

MARGARET: (*Bitterly*). Am I a slave that you can change from house to house? And from master to master against my will?

DANIEL: Didn't you tell me a while ago …?

MARGARET: What did I tell you?

BRIAN: Yes?

MARGARET: (*Raises her hands*). Oh! My heart is broken and the fault is mine. (*Stretching her hands towards her mother*). Mother, why do you look at me like that? Let me speak to Daniel. Let you all leave us.

BRIDGET: That's the best thing for us to do. Let them settle it between them. Let us go into the house.

MARY: Girl, I implore you.

BRIDGET *seizes* MARY.

BRIDGET: Come with me, Mary. Come, Brian.

BRIAN *is about to follow them, but he looks at* MARGARET *and stands. He speaks in a loud voice.*

BRIAN: Could I say a word to you first, Margaret?

MARY: Come, Brian.

BRIAN: I won't.

MARGARET: I'll have to speak to Daniel first Brian.

Pause.

BRIAN: That will do. I will go past the gable of the house until ye are finished.

BRIAN *goes behind the gable of the house. The two women enter by the door. The door is closed.* MARGARET *goes to the left of the stage. Pause.*

MARGARET: Why don't you speak to me, Daniel?

DANIEL *comes to the centre of the stage. He gazes ahead, his eyes wandering, his face twitching.*

DANIEL: I'm not a man for many words.

MARGARET: Have you nothing to say to me?

DANIEL: God! There is always something at the bottom of my throat, preventing me from talking, when I ... when I try to speak from my heart. There is a flood of words in my heart, but they are frozen. I never spoke from my heart. Milking the cow in the evening, when the birds were singing in the branches and the sweet smell of the cow was making my heart happy and the great world lying peaceful around me, I ... I ... (*He cries aloud*). I wanted to cry aloud ... but I never could.

Pause. DANIEL *is rigid.*

MARGARET: (*Approaching him*). Do you love me, Daniel?

DANIEL: (*Turning towards her*). I will work for you until the skin cracks on my hands and until my spine twists with hardship.

MARGARET: But ... but haven't you something else to say to me?

DANIEL: What? Is it about the land you ... The land is mine. Every sod of it. I believe Brian will be living in the house until ...

MARGARET: Stop! Stop!

DANIEL *approaches her trembling with outstretched hands.*

DANIEL: Margaret.

His face is wild with passion. She looks at him and she becomes afraid. She goes from him across the stage terrified. He follows her crying in an agonised voice.

DANIEL: Margaret! Margaret!

MARGARET: (*At the gable*). Brian! Come quickly. Keep away, Daniel.

DANIEL *stands.* BRIAN *rushes around the gable.* BRIAN *and* DANIEL *stare at one another.*

DANIEL: You are coming between us.

BRIAN: (*Excitedly*). I have only two words to say. Then I'll go. I'll follow my face in wandering.

DANIEL: Speak in my presence.

BRIAN: I can't. For God's sake ...

DANIEL: There is treachery in your mind.

BRIAN: Believe me, brother. It's for mother's sake.

DANIEL: Go. Go. Don't come between us.

MARY: (*Rushing from the house*). What's that? What's this?

MARGARET: (*Running towards Mary*). Bring Daniel in with you.

BRIAN: (*To Mary*). I have only two words to say.

BRIDGET *rushes out.*

MARY: Come in, Daniel. Don't refuse him.

BRIDGET: Come in, my treasure.

They bring DANIEL *into the house between them. The door is closed.* BRIAN *rushes to* MARGARET. *He takes her two hands in his and kisses them.*

BRIAN: Oh! You wonder of the world.

MARGARET: (*Throwing back her head*). Ah! God of Glory!

They look into one another's eyes.

BRIAN: Now when you are gone from me, I know that you are my sun by day and my moon brightening the night.

MARGARET: (*Softly*). I never heard that sound in your voice before. (*He bends his head over her hands. She kisses his hair. Shivering*). What question did you want to ask me?

BRIAN: Now, when you are so near me in the loneliness of the night, I have no question to ask you but one I can't ask, since you are gone from me.

MARGARET: (*Weakly*). I gone from you?

BRIAN: Gone! Gone! And I to go from you through far wandering and desolation. You are my brother's now.

MARGARET: I'm not his yet.

BRIAN: Ah! I would be a cowardly man if ... God I have ruined my life.

MARGARET: Oh! Why didn't you speak like this to me before?

BRIAN: I was jealous. I thought that ...

MARGARET: Damnation!

Pause. She sheds a tear.

MARGARET: Do you love me?

BRIAN: I love every drop of blood in your body. I feel desire in the very air that moves around you.

MARGARET: Oh! My hound of the sea! My heart and my soul belong to you. (*She puts her hands on his shoulders*). Take me with you.

BRIAN: Don't tempt me.

MARGARET: With my two hands I will wait on you. And if we have only the dome of heaven for a house I won't envy the queen in her palace. Just while you are near me. My wild fisherman!

BRIAN: (*Trying to tear himself from her*). That cannot be.

She puts her arms around his neck.

MARGARET: My warrior! Share of my heart! Take me.

BRIAN: Don't tempt me. The devil is done and we are parted.

MARGARET: Nothing can part us but death.

BRIAN: There is something worse than death.

MARGARET: What?

BRIAN: Shame.

MARGARET: You are afraid.

BRIAN: Of whom?

MARGARET: Dark Daniel.

Pause. They part. He looks at the ground.

BRIAN: It's not fear, but shame.

MARGARET *utters a little sob of contemptuous grief.*

BRIAN: You don't believe me, Margaret?

MARGARET: After all you said to me a minute ago, is not this a poor excuse you are making? Deep love swallows fear and shame in its depth. I fear nothing and I'm ashamed of nothing, Brian, while I have you near me.

BRIAN: Oh! Lord God! Yesterday or this morning I would go with you to the end of the world. But now … I curse the day I was born.

MARGARET: Oh! How cowardly are your words! You are a butterfly that is frozen with the first sharp wind of autumn. You are afraid.

BRIAN: I'm not afraid. But I love Daniel that reared me and my mother whose heart would be broken if …

MARGARET: Isn't love stronger than mother or brother? Love only comes once. Don't let it go.

BRIAN: Have pity on me. My mind is mad with horror. My pulse! Now or never I must do good for the good that has been done to me. I must suffer for their suffering. Farewell. Farewell.

They kiss fiercely.

MARGARET: Don't go. Take me.

She falls on her knees. She embraces his knees.

BRIAN: Let me go. Let me go.

He struggles away and rushes off the stage.

MARGARET: (*Reaching out after him*). Brian! Come back. Come back. I'm choking. Brian. (*She throws herself to the ground. She beats the ground with her hands. She shouts).* Come back. O! O! O!

The two women rush out of the house followed by DANIEL. *They stoop over her. They lift her up, shouting.*

THE TWO WOMEN: What's this? What's this?

MARGARET: Oh! Oh! Oh! He's gone. Bring him back.

THE TWO WOMEN: *(Leading her to the house).* Whist darling, whist!

MARGARET: Bring him back. Bring him back.

They enter the house. DANIEL *is alone on the stage. He stands, with his legs spread, squat, fierce, with his hands like claws in front of him, as if he were about to choke somebody.*

DANIEL: *(In a low savage voice).* If he comes back …

NB One minute between second and third Acts. Silence.

ACT III

SCENE:

As before. An hour later, complete darkness. MARGARET *suddenly opens the door of the house and appears on the threshold, with her hand on the latch.*

MARGARET: I'm only going out into the yard for a moment.

BRIDGET: (*From within*). Don't be long out under the cold of the night, my darling.

MARGARET *comes out, closing the door behind her. A heavy darkness has fallen. There is no moon, no stars, no sound. She looks about her at the night as she walks out over the stage.*

MARGARET: How terrible the night looks! Everything is as still as death.

She halts, listening, and gazing ahead. She sighs heavily. She strikes her forehead with her hand. She begins to tremble.

MARGARET: I wish it were death were facing me instead of ... (*She walks a few steps*). He's in there now sitting on a stool, with his hands on his knees, with his mouth open and his eyes half-shut, like a beast watching ... (*pause*) watching me. (*Pause*). Lord God! What ...? (*Suddenly*). I'll run. I'll run. But ... Where'll I run? Where? Virgin!

She starts, suddenly hearing BRIAN *enter the stage. She puts her hands to her throat.*

BRIAN: Margaret. Sht! It is I. Listen. (*He runs to her, looking towards the house fearfully. He takes her in his arms and kisses her. She lies lifelessly in his hands, with her head thrown backwards*). Share of my heart! My pulse! I had to come back. I couldn't leave you. Margaret! Speak, where are they?

MARGARET: (*Going from him*). Go! Leave me. Go. You cowardly treacherous wretch, leave me. Coming now when ... with your ...

He seizes her again fiercely and puts his hand on her mouth.

BRIAN: Stop! Stop! You'll have to come with me. I have the curragh ready on the rock. The oars are on the rowing pins. I have only to push her into the tide and be off. We'll reach the Lofty Island before the storm breaks.

MARGARET: Fool! Do you want to kill me?

BRIAN: There's no danger.

MARGARET: Be gone before ...

BRIAN: I'd die first.

MARGARET: We'll be both dead if Daniel ...

BRIAN: (*Fiercely*). Daniel! To hell with him.

MARGARET: He'll follow us.

BRIAN: He can't. He was never in a curragh and it will be a raging hurricane in half an hour.

MARGARET: Be gone.

She rushes towards the door.

BRIAN: (*Reaching for her with his hands*). If you don't come I'll be drowned with the dawn.

She halts suddenly and wheels towards him. She comes to him, running. They kiss passionately. Then suddenly a clap of thunder bursts, a dull roar, afar off. They start. There is a short pause. They are gazing ahead timorously. Then BRIDGET'S *voice is heard from within the house.*

BRIDGET: (*Within*). Come in out of that, daughter. (*They start again.* BRIAN *stoops, lifts her in his arms and rushes off the stage with her. As he stooped to lift her, his cap fell off. Another clap of thunder is heard, and then another. The door opens and* BRIDGET *appears*). God save us! The sky is cracking. Margaret! Where are you? Margaret, I say!

Pause. BRIDGET *becomes terrified.*

BRIDGET: Daughter! Where are you? Where are you? (MARY *and* DANIEL *emerge. Another clap of thunder is heard*). There is no sign of her. Oh, daughter!

DANIEL: (*Wildly*). She's gone.

MARY: Have patience. Where would she be gone?

DANIEL: (*More wildly*). She is gone with him. He came back.

BRIDGET: (*Mad with fright*). With whom? With whom, man?

DANIEL *crouches about peering at the ground, suddenly he yells.*

DANIEL: With Brian. (*He points*). Ha! Look, at his cap.

They all rush to the cap, stoop over it, lift it up between them and examine it, feeling it with their hands excitedly, as if there was some occult charm in it. Then as a clap of thunder bursts rumbling they all start and make the sign of the cross on themselves. Each undergoes a mental change. They are all carried away, differently, into a sort of ecstasy of fear, while they stand that way motionless and aghast. DANIEL suddenly begins to tremble. He is staring in front of him, but gradually his hands rise, clawing, until they are level with his shoulders. Then he darts a suspicious, cunning glance at each of the women and he retreats backwards noiselessly towards the house a few paces. Then he turns and makes for the door. The women, dazed and listening motionless, do not notice him.

BRIDGET: (*As if waking from a dream*). He was here.

MARY: He was.

They look at one another. They undergo another mental change. The stupor with which they were seized becomes active, expressing itself in a furious passion. They gaze in silence at one another, but their bodies gradually become more and more excited.

BRIDGET: (*In a sudden shout*). Now what has your brat done? My curse on him!

MARY: My share of misfortune on you! Whose fault is it but your daughter's. The shameless whore.

BRIDGET: You yellow shrivelled hag! It was an evil hour I set foot on your threshold.

MARY: I'll kill you, you she devil.

BRIDGET: There's a curse on your house.

MARY: Begone demon. If your raised your daughter properly –

BRIDGET: You heap of sloth.

MARY: And she going with her head in the air –

BRIDGET: Stuck in the ashes you where when you should be –

MARY: Pride and selfishness have been eating her –

BRIDGET: One of your sons is a lout and –

DANIEL: (*Rushing from the house with a knife in his hand*). There's going to be murder done. I'll have his life.

The two women start. They attempt to catch him as he rushes past them off the stage.

MARY: Daniel! Daniel!

DANIEL *disappears into the darkness.* MARY *begins wailing. She runs after him with her hands outstretched.* BRIDGET *pursues her and seizes her.* MARY *turns to* BRIDGET *and they embrace one another. Then they both begin to lament in the mode of the lamentation for the dead, the sound of their voices rising and falling in a sort of artificial rhythm.*

BRIDGET: Oc-oc-ochon! my beautiful daughter, my bright treasure!

MARY: Oc-oc-ochon! My children! My children, I am terrified.

BRIDGET: Whither, whither shall I go to find her; whither shall I turn my face in the morning?

Another thunder clap is heard. The women part. They move to and fro across the stage wailing.

MARY: I am accursed. I am accursed.

BRIDGET: Oc-oc-ochon, my little Margaret.

MARY: Oh! I am forlorn and I ...

BRIDGET: Pearl of my heart and you have gone from me.

MARY: And nobody left me in the end of my life.

BRIDGET: In the darkness of the world I will be in anguish.

MARY: Murder and drowning and I wailing.

BRIDGET: The sky being bent and you wandering.

MARY: Suffering, suffering and sorrow.

BRIDGET: Far wandering and the destruction of the sea.

MARY: Oc-oc-ochon, my two bright sons.

BRIDGET: Oc-oc-ochon, my merry daughter.

They meet. Three claps of thunder burst almost simultaneously in three different quarters of the sky. MARY *raises her hands to heaven.* BRIDGET *seizes her by the bosom.*

MARY: Burst now you devil. Spill. Burst. Tear.

BRIDGET: (*Aghast with fear*). Don't! God! Mercy!

MARY: I will. I will. My curse on the world. Spill. Burst. Tear. Fall. Fall. (*Screaming*). Fall.

BRIDGET: (*Shrinking from her*). She is mad.

MARY: (*Pursuing her*). She witch, you are the cause of it. But I have you now.

BRIDGET *screams. She turns rapidly from* MARY. MARY *pursues her heavily.* BRIDGET *rushes to the edge of the stage. Just as she is about to disappear she halts, gasps and throws up her hands. Then she retreats a pace.* BRIAN *and* MARGARET *stumble on to the stage, clasping one another. The two women cry aloud.*

THE TWO WOMEN: Woe! Woe!

BRIAN: (*Whispering*). Who is here?

BRIDGET: Margaret.

MARGARET *runs to her mother. They kiss.*

MARY: My little Brian!

BRIAN: (*Whispering*). Where is Daniel?

MARY: (*Ordering him off with her hands*). My little son! Run! Run! He is tracking you.

BRIAN: (*Waving his hands in the air*). Whither? The curragh was swept from the rock. The sea rose in one wave. There's only white froth between the two islands.

MARY: Run, my son.

BRIAN: Whither?

MARGARET *leaves her mother and rushes to* BRIAN.

MARGARET: Don't leave me.

BRIAN: Never!

MARY: (*To* MARGARET). Let him go.

BRIDGET: (*Catches* MARGARET). Let him go. Come away.

MARGARET: Never. Brian, take me away.

BRIAN: Protect us mother. Where is he?

MARY: Leave her to him. Hide among the caverns of the dead forest. Let her go. Let her go.

BRIDGET: Come, Margaret.

MARGARET: I won't. Come, Brian.

Suddenly a yell is heard from DANIEL. *They all scream.* BRIAN *rushes towards the door.* DANIEL *rushes on to the stage, with his knife poised, in pursuit of* BRIAN. *The three women try to stop* DANIEL. *He darts past them.* BRIAN *enters the house.* DANIEL *plunges in after him. The women gasp. There is a moment's pause. Then a low agonising cry is heard from* BRIAN. *Then there is a heavy thud. The women are rigid. Then* DANIEL'S *voice is heard.*

DANIEL: (*Within*). Ha! Ha! Ha!

The women scream and rush to the door. They enter. Loud cries are heard. Then DANIEL'S *voice is heard again.*

DANIEL: (*Within*). He is killed now.

Absolute silence. Then a low moaning sound rises from the house. The three women are wailing over the dead body. DANIEL *staggers forth from the door, holding the bloody knife in his hand. The moaning sound increases.*

MARGARET: (*Subdued voice*). Your little dead hand is in my hand.

MARY: Oc-oc-ochon.

BRIDGET: Oc-oc-ochon.

When their voices are heard DANIEL *staggers to the left front of the stage. He peers into the darkness. He cries aloud.*

DANIEL: (*Aloud*). Darkness!

He staggers towards the right of the stage.

MARGARET: (*More subdued*). My heart is frozen in me ...

MARY: Oc-oc-ochon ...

BRIDGET: Oc-oc-ochon ...

DANIEL *reaches the right of the stage. He peers ahead into the darkness. He cries.*

DANIEL: (*More subdued and as if he were choking*). Darkness!

He staggers over to the centre front of the stage.

MARGARET: (*Almost inaudible*). Take me with you to the grave.

MARY: (*Almost inaudible*). Oc-oc-ochon.

BRIDGET: (*Almost inaudible*). Oc-oc-ochon.

DANIEL *is at the front of the stage. He cries.*

DANIEL: (*Still more subdued*). Darkness!

There is perfect silence. DANIEL *begins to retreat to the door. His figure begins to crumble up and he is protecting his face with his left hand, while in the right hand he holds the bloody knife. He suddenly stiffens. He halts. Then he sinks down to the earth, crying out three times as he sinks.*

DANIEL: (*Low*). Darkness! (*Lower*). Darkness! (*Still lower*). Darkness!

He lies prostrate.

CURTAIN

1. *The Irish Times*, 2 March 1926, 5.
2. *Irish Statesman*, 6 March 1926, 802.
3. *Fáinne an Lae*, 13 March 1926, 6.
4. *Fáinne an Lae*, 13 March, 1926, 6.

1. Gaelic Plays at the Abbey Theatre, *The Irish Times* 2 March 1926, 5.

"Last night's performance by the Gaelic Players at the Abbey Theatre was attended by a good deal of curiosity; for the play of the evening was the first production of a three-act tragedy *Dorchadas*, by Liam O'Flaherty. It proved to be exceedingly interesting and it was somewhat surprising to find a novelist proving himself so well skilled in stagecraft: for the play was wholly free from amateur weakness. The chief weakness in *Darkness* – as the play is called – is that it inevitably reminds us of *Birthright*, – for it has a closely similar theme – jealousy among brothers, issuing in tragedy. It was finely staged last night. The characters in the romantic Western fisherfolk's attire familiarised by Synge's plays, were vivid and convincing, and their language had a native eloquence, more satisfying than Synge's unreal diction. The elder brother (M. Ó Catháin), dour and suspicious, the toiler of the family, seems to be preferred by the girl (Máire Ní Oisín), who tells the gay, poetic younger son that she prefers the sinewy hand of the man to the soft palm of the boy. Now, the mother of the boys and the girl's mother discuss the proposed match, and favour the claim of the elder son; but the younger claims the right to make a final plea. Left alone, the elder son makes a poor weper (sic). Our interest is fixed on the girl's wavering choice. After the elder brother comes the younger, and we are shown the girl, already weakened by his downcast manner, carried away now by his words, flaming with Gaelic eloquence. She agrees to fly with him. The final scene is set in a terrible Western storm. From the cottage on the ocean's brink, amid lightning flashes, the young couple appear. They are pursued by the older brother, whose jealousy has loosened the passions of a dumb soul. He pursues the younger brother with a skian; they enter the cottage; like the Greek chorus at the slaying of Agamemnon within the walls, the women raise the terrible Western keen. The murderer emerges – demented. As the mother of the boys, Máire Ní Shíocháin made the mistake of beginning on too high a note, leaving herself no reserves; but she was impressive. As the girl's mother, Máire Ní Chinnéide was exceedingly good – sympathetic, and even majestic – Máire Ní Oisín was not too well cast for the girl's part which needed subtler treatment of emotion. The second play was Mrs. Constance Powell-Anderson's ever delightful little comedy *Wooing the Widow*; and here Máire Ní Oisín, as a roguish girl, who helps the lovers to woo in poetry, is at her best. Mr. Ó Scanaill was welcome in his old part of the fierce wooer. The piece is among the best in the players' repertoire.

2. 'Oscar Óg', 'The Gaelic Players', *Irish Statesman* 6 Márta 1926, 802.

On Monday night the Gaelic Players played two plays before a full house. The first was a three-act tragedy by Liam O'Flaherty which is rightly entitled *Gloom*. Though the play may be faulty in many ways, yet it is encouraging to find original work of such promise being done. The scene is presumably in the Aran Islands and we have before us the eternal tragedy of two brothers and one girl. There is a sharp contrast between Gloomy

Dan the farmer and Laughing Brian the fisherman. The mother makes a match for Gloomy Dan, but alas the girl loves his more cheerful brother. She wants Brian to flee with her, but he has a conscience and is reluctant, though madly in love with her. In the third act they decide to flee, but as they start off in the coracle, a fearful storm breaks out and they are driven back only to meet the furious Dan, knife in hand. Brian is killed and Dan, realizing now what he has done, falls dead from shock. They play has two faults: firstly, there is a feeling that too much has been done in a short space – it needs and could bear elaboration – and, secondly, it lacks dignity, especially in the third act. Here it is dangerously near melodrama, and needs more careful treatment not to be even funny in parts. The actors must be excused, for the play was produced at extremely short notice, but Máire Ní Shíocháin, who played the rather thankless role of the mother, could greatly improve her part if she allowed herself more crescendo instead of becoming fortissimo immediately. Muiris Ó Catháin and Gearóid Ó Lochlainn, who played the parts of Dan and Brian, deserve great praise. The second play, a slight comedy, *Flirting with the Widow*, was extremely well played by all the cast, notably Máire Ní Oisín and Máire Ní Shíocháin.

3. Neol. An *Dorchadas*, *Fáinne an Lae* 13 Márta 1926, 6.**

Bhítheas ag fanúint go mí-fhoighdeach le céad léiriú *Dorchadas* – dráma bunaidh ag Liam Ó Flaithbeartaigh (*sic*) – agus nuair a cuireadh ar an stáitse é bhí Amharclann na Mainistreach lán go doras amach. Bhí fáth leis an mí-fhoighid óir is duine an Flaithbheartach a bhfuil clú i bhfad is i ngearr air mar gheall ar a shaothar i litridheacht an Bhéarla agus ar sgríobh sé le goirid de ghearrsgéalta Gaedhilge ar *Fáinne an Lae*. Shásuigh an léiriú mí-fhoighid agus suim neamh-choitcianta an lucht éisteachta.

An sgéal is ádhbhar do'n dráma, thiar i n-Oileáin Árann a thuiteas sé amach. Beirt dearbhráthar agus cailín – seansgéal atá caithte go maith faoi'n am seo. Ach i n-inneóin a sheanda is tá an sgéal d'éirigh leis an ughdar caraictéireacht thar na bearta a dhéanamh ar fhuirinn an dráma ar chuma go raibh coladh na nódhachta ar ghach aon phioc de tríd síos. Dráma ealadhanta é go mb'fhearrde litridheacht na Gaedhilge a lán eile dá shórt a bheith ar fáil.

Tar éis an léirighthe fheiceál fanann pictiúirí áirithe i n-aigne duine. Fanann tuairim ar an dráma ina iomláine nach féidir a cheilt ach fanann le hais na tuairime pictiúirí nó dealbha áirithe a réidhtigheas le dath an dráma agus nach réidhtighean. Ní fhéadfaí, cuir i gcás, a mhalairt de theidil a thabhairt air: Dorchadas. Ní raibh léas solais ann ó thosach go deire marab' é gealgháire Bhriain é sa gcéad mhír agus géarmhagadh Mhaighréid Uaibhrigh. Ach sníomhan an sgéal i n-aon crescendo uamhain amháin ó árdhuightear an brat go dtuitean sé ar chorpán an dearbhráthar is sine fá dheire thiar.

Beidh daoine an a déarfas leat nár thaithnigh gruaim an dráma leó ach níl aoinne a déarfadh nár thaithnigh ealadhantacht an dráma leo. Níl cleachtadh ag Gaedhilgeóirí ar dhrámaí dá leithéid seo – saghas nuadh iad i reanna na litridheachta – agus is féidir le Gaedhilgeóirí bheith cinnte gur minic feasta a fheicfeas siad a macsamhla. Tá treóir ag sgríbhneóirí Gaedhilge i dtrom-dhrámuíocht anois nach raibh aca go dtí seo. Is fad ó thug Piaras Béaslaí eolas dúinn ar cheird an dráma éadtruim grinn agus is féidir a thabhairt fá deara ar na drámaí grinn a lean drámaí Phiarais Bhéaslaí go rabhthas ag déanamh aithrise ar chreata agus ar mhodhtha comhráidh an úghdair sin. Ach i bpáirt na ndrámaí bróin nó na dtraigéidí b'éigean do'n Chomhar bheith i dtuilleamh-mbuidhe aistriúchán. Beidh atharrú ar an sgéal sin amach annseo. Tá giota eile de'n bhóthar curtha dhínn againn.

Ní dráma sanntach *Dorchadas*, .i. ní baintear fad gan gádh as. Tá dóthain smaointe ann chun é shíneadh ach bhí an ceart ag an bhFlaithbheartach na smaointe seo a dhingeadh isteach ar a chéile go neamh-thrócaireach i gcás go mba mhóide uathbhás a chríche. Traosluighim do'n Ghaedhilge eolaidhe cliste cumasach a bheith ag baint feadhma aistí mar mheadhon drámata.

Maidir leis an aithriseóireacht agus an aisteóireacht níor buadhadh ariamh roimhe orra. Ní féidir idir-dhealú do dhéanamh idir na hAisteóirí ach ceadóchar dom má deirim focailín fá leith i n-onóir Mhuiris Uí Chatháin. Bhí sé go hiongantach. Ní beag sin.

4. Theo. *Dorchadas* – Tuairim Eile, *Fáinne an Lae* 13 Márta 1926, 6.**

A Chara, Do casadh cara liom tráthnóna Dia Luain agus bhuail an bheirt againn isteach i nAmharclann na Mainistreach. Bhí an áit lán ce's muite de chor shuidheachán in airde an staighre. Ní raibh ann ach go raibh muid in am, mar ba ghearr an t-achar gur buaileadh an 't-oighean,' gur mchadh na soillse, agus gur staideadh den chainnt. Ní raibh giog le cloisint.

D'fhanmuid 'nar dtost gur thit an brat tar éis an chéadradhairc. Céard do mheas? arsa mise: 'Tá an Ghaedhilg go deas,' ar seisean, 'agus is cosúil ón leagan cainte agus an chuma atá ortha gur ar mhuinntir Árainn atá an t-ughdar ag déanamh aithris. Cinnte is aisteach an bodach Domhnall, ach tá sé beagáinín mínádúrtha do réir mo thuairme-se.'

Buaileadh an 't-oighean' arís agus isteach linn. Ní raibh sa dara radharc ach míniú agus léiriú níos fearr ar an gcéad radharc. Ní dóigh liomsa go raibh sé ag teastáil chor ar bith. Tá sé níos soiléire ón ghníomh seo nach bhfuil i nDomhnall, ach duine gan chroidhe, gan anam, duine atá cho tugtha sin don fheirg agus nach ceart duine.

D'fanmuid leis an treas ghníomh. Bhí chuile dhuine agus cluas air ach bhí bualadh bos le cloisint anois agus arís faoi rud eicínt uathbhásach. Daoine a shíl gur thuig siad, ach nár thuig. Fá cheann tamaillín d'áirigh mé glór fir ar mo chúl, 'Bog díom! bog díom, adeirim!' D'fhéach mé thart agus chonnaic mé gur cailín a bhí ann agus greim ghuailne aicí ar an bhfear a bhí ag cainnt. D'fhoscail sí a súile agus dubhairt sí go faiteach creathach, 'Gabhaim pardún agat, ní raibh neart agam air mar gur sgannruigheadh chomh mór sin mé nuair a chonnaic mé an sgian. Ar marbhuigheadh an bheirt óg?' Thuit an brat agus amach linn.

"'Dar-! An féidir linn ughdar maith Gaedhilge 'fháil agus a bhéas ina Chríostuidhe san am chéanna? Tá adhbhar an drama chomh sean leis an gceo. Ach na hainmneacha 'athrú seo sgéal an drama. ?Do chomhraig Domhnall ré na dhearbhráthair Brian: agus thárla ann a nuair do bhádar ar an teallach gur éirigh Domhnall suas a naghuidh a dhearbhrathar agus gur mhairbh é; óir do bhádar éadmhar a los mná.'

Gan aimhreas ar bith is duairc dorcha na hintinn atá ag cuid d'ár scríobhnóirí. Tá duairceas agus dorchadas na Rúise ag ithe isteach 'na gcroidhthe. Is mór an dul amú atá ar an úghdar má cheapann sé gur mar sin a mhaireann muinntir an Iarthair ná más smaointe den tsórt sin a bhíos acú. Dorchadas a aigne féin atá á léiriú ag an úghdar, tá faitchíos orm.

Tá a intinn ag imirt cleas air mar d'imrigh intinn Singe cleas air agus é a scríobh dráma in atmosphere an Iarthair. Níl i nDomhnall dorcha ach Playboy eile. Mar dhrama, níl a fhios agam an ceart drama bróin a thabhairt air no melodrama. Ní réiteochadh an dráma le tuairim an phágánaigh Aristotle féin. Ní thig leis an ughdar a rá go bhfuil Katharsis an Ghréigigh le feiceál ann. Sén fáth go scríobhtar drama bróin chor ar bith ná le anam an duine do ghlanadh tré fhaitchíos a chur air sa gcaoi go mbeadh truaigh aige don chuirpeach. Mar dubhairt an Franncach ní mór une douce terreur et une pitié charmanta chun drama bróin do dhéanamh. Ba cheart go dtuigfeadh an t-éisteoir go bhféadfadh go dtagadh an mí-ádh céanna air féin i gcás den tsórt céanna. Annsin ní mór trauigh a bheith ag an éisteoir do'n chuirpeach. Cé aige a mbeadh truaigh do chuirpeach a mharbhuigheann a dhearbhrathair mar gheall ar ghirrsigh (a bhanchéile?) Ní ceist grádh é chor ar bith mar ní thuigeann Domhnall rud ar bith faoi ghrádh cé gurbh í seo a chaint féin: déanfa mé mo ghearán leis na hainmhidhe beaga atá ag gruasgar i bhféar na páirce. Níl aon mhuintreas agam-sa leis an gcine daondha: bóránach basach mé.' Cén mhaith do dhaoine a bheith ag leigint ortha gurb ionann muinntir Árainn agus 'bóránach basach' a chruthuigh an t-ughdhar as a inntinn ghruamdha, dhorcha, féin? Ollphiast den tsórt a cheap Emily Bronte atá i gceist aige, ach níor leig sise uirthí gur mhair a leithéid de chuirpeach ariamh. Ní fearracht sin ar ár scríobhnóirí Gaedhilge – agus Béarla – 'má tá ollphiast i gceist agat abair gur as Árainn a tháinig sé!'

Níl de dhorchadas i gcroidhthe na ndaoine gur uatha a shíolruigh an t-ughdar ach an dorchadas atá i gcroidhthe Críostuidhthe, agus tuigtear go bhfuil níos mó measa acú ar dhlighthe Dé ná cheapann an t-úghdar in a intinn shuaraigh féin.

Sgaramar le n-a chéile annsin, agus chuaidh mé abhaile agus gheallas dá mbeadh drama den tsort sin uaim arís go rachann go dtí an Queen's***, áit nach leigfeadh na hughdair ortha gur as an nGaeltacht gach sórt cuirpeach a bheadh luaidhte sa drama. Theo.

* Carachtar ó mhiotaseolaíocht na Gréige. Tar éis thurnamh Traoi, tugadh an spéirbhean Cassandra d'Agamemon mar éadáil catha, ach mharaigh Aegisthus agus Clytaemnestra, bean chéile Agamemnon, iad nuair a d'fhill siad ón gcath.

** Níor leasaíodh litriú ná gramadach an ailt seo. Buaileadh cló iodálach ar théarmaí iasachta.

*** The Queen's Royal Theatre, nó Queen's mar ab fhearr aithne air i measc an phobail. Tógadh é ar Shráid Brunswick (Sráid an Phiarsaigh anois) Téatar in 1844. Bhí cáil air mar ionad do cheoltóirí, d'amhránaithe agus d'fhuirseoirí. Deineadh athchóiriú ar an bhfoirgneamh in 1893. Is ann a bhí Amharclann na Mainistreach lonnaithe idir na blianta 1951–1966.

Leagadh an téatar in 1969 agus tógadh Teach an Phiarsaigh ina áit, atá mar chuid de Choláiste na Tríonóide anois.

BIBLIOGRAPHY

Allen, Nicholas. 2009. *Modernism, Ireland and Civil War*. Cambridge University Press.

Béaslaí, Piaras. 1957. 'Stephen MacKenna: A Conversation', *Irish Times*. 15 November, 5.

Breathnach, Diarmuid & Ní Mhurchú, Máire, 1986. *1882–1982: Beathaisnéis a hAon*. Baile Átha Cliath: An Clóchomhar Tta.

Breathnach, Diarmuid & Ní Mhurchú, Máire. 1992. *1882–1982: Beathaisnéis a Trí*. Baile Átha Cliath: An Clóchomhar Tta.

Byrne, Patrick. n.d. 'Dublin Pubs' in Tom Kennedy (ed.). *Dublin*. Dublin: Albertine Kennedy Publishing.

Bronski, Michael. 2002. 'Hero with a dirty face', *The Boston Phoenix*. 15 August.

Cahalan, James M. 1991. *Liam O'Flaherty: A Study of the Short Fiction*. Boston: Twayne Publishers.

Cahalan, James M. 1993. *Modern Irish Literature and Culture: A Chronology*. New York: G.K. Hall & Co.

Conneely, Mairéad. 2011. *Between Two Shores/Idir Dhá Chladach: Writing the Aran Islands, 1890–1980*. Oxford: Peter Lang AG.

Costello, Peter. 1996. *Liam O'Flaherty's Ireland*. Dublin: Wolfhound Press.

Cronin, John. 2003. 'Liam O'Flaherty and Dúil', *New Hibernia Review/Iris Éireannach Nua*, 7.1: 45–55.

de Bhaldraithe, Tomás. 1967. 'Liam Ó Flaitheartha: Aistritheoir', *Comhar*, May, 26.

de Bhaldraithe, Tomás. 1968. 'Liam O'Flaherty – Translator (?)' *Éire-Ireland* 3.2: 149–53.

De hAe, Risteárd. 1940. *Clár Litridheacht na Nua-Ghaeilge 1850– 1936*, III, Baile Átha Cliath. Oifig Dhíolta Foilseacháin Rialtais.

Denvir, Gearóid. 1991. *An Dúil is Dual*. Indreabhán, Gaillimh: Cló Iar Chonnachta.

Denvir, Gearóid. 1978. *Aistí Phádraic Uí Chonaire*. Gaillimh: Cló Chois Fharraige.

Doyle, Paul A. 1971. *Liam O'Flaherty*. New York: Twayne Publishers, Inc.

Doyle, Paul. A. 1972. *Liam O'Flaherty: An Annotated Bibliography*. Try, New York: The Whitston Publishing Company Inc.

Elborn, Geoffrey. 1990. *Francis Stuart: A Life*. Dublin: Raven Arts Press.

'Eoin'. 1926. *Irish Independent*. 3 March, 8.

Fox, R.M. 1938. *Smoky Crusade.* Hogarth Press, 180–8.

Fox, R.M. 1943. *History of the Irish Citizen Army.* Dublin: James Duffy & Co.

Goodway, D. 1977. 'Charles Lahr: Anarchist, Bookseller'. *London Magazine,* June-July, 47–55.

Hartley, L.P. 1926. 'New Fiction'. *The Saturday Review,* 13 November, 592.

Higgins, Michael D. 1985. 'Liam O'Flaherty & Peadar O'Donnell: Images of Rural Community'. *The Crane Bag,* 9.1: 41–8.

Hiliard, Christopher. 2005. 'Modernism and the Common Writer'. *The Historical Journal,* 48.3: 769–87.

Hillard, Christopher. 2006. 'Producers by Hand and by Brain: Working-Class Writers and Left-Wing Publishers in 1930s Britain'. *The Journal of Modern History,* 78.1: 37–64.

Hoult, Norah. 1934. 'Liam O'Flaherty and the Irish Scene'. *The Bookman.* 170.

Hudson, Mark. 2007. 'Lost Treasures of the British Picasso'. *The Telegraph.* 13 January.

Krause, David. 1980. *The Letters of Sean O'Casey. Vol. 11 1942–1954.* New York. Macmillan Publishing Co., Inc.

Kelly, A.A. 1996. *The Letters of Liam O'Flaherty.* Dublin: Wolfhound Press.

Lahr, Sheila. *Yealm.* http://www.militantesthetix.co.uk/yealm/CONTENTS.htm

Lahr, Sheila. 2011. Private correspondence with Brian Ó Conchubhair.

Lloyd, David. 1999. *Ireland after History.* Cork: Cork University Press.

Lynch, Brendan. 2011. *Prodigals & Geniuses.* Dublin: The Liffey Press.

Mac an Iomaire, Liam. 2000. *Breandán Ó hEithir: Iomramh Aonair.* Indreabhán: Cló Iar-Chonnachta.

Mac Congáil, Nollaig. 1981. 'Nóta faoi Shaothar Gaeilge Liam Uí Fhlaithearta'. *Comhar,* 40.6: 17.

Mac Congáil, Nollaig. 2003. *Na Blianta Corracha.* Scríbhinní Mháire 2. Coiscéim

McMahon, Timothy. 2008. *Grand Opportunity: The Gaelic Revival and Irish Society 1893–1910.* Syracuse. Syracuse University Press.

'M.A.T.' 1926. 'Stage and Platform'. *Sunday Independent*. 7 March, 2.

Ní Chionnaith, Eibhlín. 1995. *Pádraic Ó Conaire: Scéal a Bheatha*. Indreabhán: Cló Iar-Chonnachta.

Ní Chnáimhín, A. 1947. *Pádraic Ó Conaire*. Baile Átha Cliath: Oifig an tSoláthair.

Ní Mhuircheartaigh, Éadaoin & Mac Congáil, Nollaig. 2008. *Drámaí Thús na hAthbheochana*. Galway: Arlen House.

Ní Mhurchú, Máire & Breathnach, Diarmuid. 2007. *Beathaisnéis a Naoi: Forlíonadh agus Innéacsanna*. Baile Átha Cliath: An Clóchomhar Tta.

'Noel', 1926. *Fáinne an Lae*, 13 March, 2.

O'Brien, James H. 1973. *Liam O'Flaherty*. Lewisburg: Bucknell University Press.

Ó Broin, León. n.d. ... *Just like Yesterday: An Autobiography*. Dublin: Gill & Macmillan.

Ó Cathasaigh, Aindrias. 2007. *Réabhlóid Phádraic Uí Chonaire*. Baile Átha Cliath: Coiscéim.

Ó Cathasaigh, Aindrias. 2009. *Ré Nua os comhair na nGael? Conspóidí Chonradh na Gaeilge 1932–1939*. Baile Átha Cliath: Coiscéim.

Ó Conaire, Pádraic. 1918. 'Drámaí', *The Irishman*. 28 September.

Ó Conchubhair, Brian. 2000. 'Liam Ó Flaithearta agus Scríobh na Gaeilge: Ceist Airgid nó Cinneadh Chonradh na Gaeilge?', *New Hibernia Review/Iris Éireannach Nua*, 4.2: 116–140.

Ó Conchubhair, Brian. 2011. 'An Gúm, The Free State and the Politics of the Irish Language'. Linda King & Elaine Sisson (eds.) *Ireland, Design and Visual Culture: Negotiating Modernity, 1922–1992*. Cork: Cork University Press. 93–113.

Ó Donghaile, Deaglán. 2011. *Blasted Literature: Victorian Political Fiction and the Shock of Modernism*. Edinburgh University Press.

O'Donovan, Michael. 1934. 'Two Languages', *The Bookman*, 240–1.

Ó hAnluain, Eoghan. 1984. 'A writer who bolstered the Irish revival'. *Irish Times*, 8 September, 7.

Ó hEithir, Breandán. 1977. 'Liam Ó Flatharta agus a Dhúchas'. *Willie the Plain Pint agus an Pápa*. Corcaigh. Cló Mercier , 65–76.

Ó hEithir, Breandán. 1987. *A Guide to History, Politics & Culture*. Dublin: O'Brien Press.

O'Flaherty, Liam. 1927. *The Life of Tim Healy*. London: Jonathan Cape, 1927.

O'Flaherty, Liam. 1927. 'Writing in Gaelic'. *Irish Statesman*, 17 December, 348.

O'Flaherty, Liam. 1946. 'Irish Revival Delights Liam O'Flaherty'. *Irish Press*, 13 May, 4.

Ó Flaitheartha, Liam. 1953. 'Pádraic Ó Conaire'. *Comhar*, April. reprinted in Tomás de Bhaldraithe (ed.), *Pádraic Ó Conaire: Clocha ar a Charn*. Baile Átha Cliath. An Clóchomhar Tta., 51–7.

Ó Glaisne, Risteárd. 1980. 'Rogha Teanga: Ó Flaithearta agus an Ghaeilge', *Comhar*, 39.6: 16–7.

O'Leary, Philip. 2004. *Gaelic Prose in the Irish Free State 1922–1939*. Dublin. University College Dublin Press.

'Oscar Óg', 1926. *Irish Statesman*, 6 March, 802.

Ó Siadhail, Pádraig. 1989. *Bairbre Rua agus Drámaí Eile*. Indreabhán: Cló Iar-Chonnachta.

Ó Siadhail, Pádraig. 1993. *Stair Dhrámaíocht na Gaeilge 1900–1970*. Indreabhán: Cló Iar-Chonnachta.

Ó Siadhail, Pádraig. 2007. *An Béaslaíoch: Beatha agus Saothar Phiarais Béaslaí (1881–1965)*. Baile Átha Cliath: Coiscéim.

Ó Súilleabháin, Donnchadh. 1972. 'Tús agus Fás na Drámaíochta i nGaeilge'. *Ardán*. Summer, 2–11.

Ó Tuathaigh, Gearóid. 2008. 'The State and the Irish Language' in Caoilfhionn Nic Pháidín agus Seán Ó Cearnaigh. *A New View of the Irish Language*. Baile Átha Cliath: Cois Life, 26–42.

Pearse, P.H. 1906. 'About Literature'. *An Claidheamh Soluis*, 26 May.

Savage, Robert J. 2010. *A loss of innocence?: Television and Irish Society 1960–72*. Manchester: Manchester University Press.

Sheeran, Patrick F. 1976. *The Novels of Liam O'Flaherty: A Study in Romantic Realism*. Atlantic Highlands, New Jersey: Humanities Press.

Sheeran, Pat. 1984. 'Beastly Loot'. *Comhar*. 43.12: 40–2.

Shepherd-Barr, Kirsten. E. 2010. 'Staging Modernism' in Peter Brooker (ed.) *Oxford Handbook of Modernisms*. Oxford University Press. 122–138.

Sisson, Elaine. 2010. 'A Note on What Happened' Experimental Influences on the Irish Stage: 1919–1929. *Forum Kritika* 15: 132–148.

Riggs, Pádraigín. 1994. *Pádraic Ó Conaire: Deoraí*. Baile Átha Cliath: An Clóchomhar Tta.

Ryan, W.P. 1913. 'Synge and the Irish Theatre'. *The Bookman*, December, 170–1.

Ryan, W.P. 1929. 'Drama and Democracy'. *The Bookman*, August, 271.

Shone, Richard. 1992. 'Exhibition Reviews: London and Leeds, William Roberts; Mark Gertler'. *The Burlington Magazine*, 134.1071: 394–5.

Ryan, James. 2004. 'Inadmissible Departures: Why Did the Emigrant Experience Feature so Infrequently in the Fiction of the Mid-Twentieth Century?' in D. Keogh, F. O'Shea and C. Quinlan (eds), *Ireland: The Lost Decade in the 1950s*. Cork: Mercier Press.

'Splannc'. 1926. *An Sguab*. April, 64.

Taylor, D.J. 2007. *Bright Young People: The Lost Generation of London's Jazz Age*. New York: Farrar, Straus and Giroux.

'Theo', 1926. *Fáinne an Lae*. 13 March, 2.

Tuama, Keith. 1987. 'Wyndham Lewis, Blast and Popular Culture.. *ELH*, 54.2: 403–19.

Thacker, Andrew. 2010. 'London: Rhymers, Imagists, and Vorticists' in Peter Brooker (ed.) *Oxford Handbook of Modernisms*. Oxford University Press. 687–705.

Ua Mathghamhna, Eoin. 1924. 'Obscenity in Modern Irish Literature'. *The Irish Monthly*, 52.617: 569–73.

Walsh, John. 2002. *Díchoimisiúnú Teanga: Coimisiún na Gaeltachta 1926*. Baile Átha Cliath: Cois Life.

W.B.W. 1920. 'Literary Gossip'. *The Athenaeum*, 13 August, 213.

Zimmer, John. 1970. *The Literary Vision of Liam O'Flaherty*. Syracuse: Syracuse University Press.

1930. 'A Letter from Dublin'. *Saturday Review*, 8 March, 290.

1926. *Irish Times*, 2 March, 5.

1921. 'Novels in Brief'. *The Athenaeum*, 14 January, 43.

1926. 'This Week's News of Ireland'. *Irish Times*, 1 May, 12.

ARCHIVAL SOURCES

An Gúm. File G 233/221 & G99/52

British National Archives, File WO/372/7